FIFTY WAYS I SCREWED UP MY LIFE AND HOW YOU CAN AVOID THIS

FRANÇOIS DE WAAL

CONTENTS

FOREWORD

"Without philosophy, your soul is sick"

– Seneca

I have made every mistake a person can make. I was easily irritated, spent endless hours brooding, thought constantly that I was hard done by, placed the blame on all and sundry, and was never satisfied. I was my own worst enemy and spent every day sabotaging things for myself. This caused a non-stop nagging pain, but I kept on making the same mistakes. And yet I thought I was really smart. How stupid can you get?

We are taught everything – reading, writing, arithmetic, even algebra – but not how to live. So, you live like your parents, your neighbours, people on television: moody and anxious, unrealistic, irresponsible, and full of self-pity. You are your own worst enemy. It is like never having learned to swim. As if life were an enormous swimming pool, deep and beautiful, but you can't swim: you flounder about, you don't enjoy yourself, you stand on the edge shivering, and if you do take the plunge, you drown.

If you think that you are able to learn some things – such as tying your shoelaces – but not how to live, I won't try to convince you otherwise. Just carry on living the way you are now.

But if you really want to learn something: there is hope, there is a solution! You can call it philosophy, wisdom, religion, spirituality or the art of living. I call it personal growth. This book is about personal growth. What is that? Personal growth gives answers to questions such as: What do you do with all that brooding? What do you do with all that thinking you're a failure? Thinking that you're a victim, thinking that you must always have more, thinking that life is crap and that your relationship and your work will never be enjoyable? The answers to all these questions can be found in this book.

I'm not the first person to have said these things. Writers, philosophers, and even psychologists have been telling us how you can live life to the fullest and get the most out of yourself. This book, therefore, contains nothing new.

I used to think of personal growth as a pleasant bonus, something like an after-dinner snack. It was great – but I could do without it. Now I know that without personal growth, without living consciously each day and trying to make the best of it, your life is a difficult path, littered with egotism, self-sabotage, silent despair, and years of muddling on without any light at the end of the tunnel.

Most people live unconsciously; they just do things automatically and thus fall into every trap. Their house is on fire, but they act as if nothing is happening. If they are really honest, then they may see and smell the fire, but they deny its existence, or they say: I can't do anything about it.

You can do everything about it. What's more: you must do something about it. Otherwise things will go completely and utterly wrong.

I am not a psychologist and have no clients about whom to tell anecdotes. I have been through all this misery myself, have learned all these life lessons by myself. So I thought: let me take myself as an example. This book is about personal growth. I have described fifty major traps. Plus all the solutions. I know that the problems are real, because they were and often still are my own problems. And I know that the solutions are real and work, because they are my own solutions. The tips at the end of each chapter are tips that have helped me, not tips from some handbook on psychology.

Several chapters overlap. The texts do not stand alone but rather complement and reference each other. Sometimes you see the same problem from different perspectives and hopefully this makes it clearer. You can read the book from beginning to end, but it is better to read the chapters that appeal to you. Certainly don't try to tackle every problem at the same time. Take them one by one, as I did.

Fourteen of these chapters have previously been published in Psychology Magazine. I was amazed at how many people reacted. People of all ages, educations, and backgrounds, yet all used the same word: recognisable.

This book may deal with me, but if I really thought that these problems were unique to me, I would never have written about them. This book is also about you, the reader. We are all the same and all face the same problems.

Personal growth isn't "nice" or even handy; it is essential. If you don't learn to swim, you'll drown. Without the art of living, without personal growth, you will do everything wrong and die a slow death. It is not a nice little extra, but the only way to find peace in this life.

François de Waal, Amsterdam

www.francoisdewaal.nl

"Above all, don't forget to observe your own mind. Seek out the root of the insanity there."

Eckhart Tolle, *The Power of Now*

"What is most personal is most universal."

Carl R. Rogers, *On Becoming a Person: A Therapist's View of Psychotherapy*

1 ANGRY

"Damn it, I'm not angry!"

People often asked me: "Why do you look so angry?" And I would always answer: "I'm not angry!" But they said it too often. I am angry! I'm angry about what happened in my youth. And about what didn't happen. I'm angry that I was rejected and laughed at and I'm angry that I didn't bat an eyelid.

Didn't anybody see that I was slowly dying? Isn't that why you were given parents? And teachers? Why was I good for so long? Why didn't I shout out that I was lonely and desperate and that I would have so liked an arm around my shoulder and a kick up my backside? Perhaps I was offered it, but attention was so foreign to me that I pushed it away.

Okay – enough misery. I simply want to say that I felt very bad for a long time and never expressed my anger about it. At home, anger was taboo. I never said anything and when I entered puberty, I exploded with all that unresolved anger and took my revenge. I started saying and doing things that all the people who had (had) power over me – my parents and their substitutes, the teachers, the authorities – hated. I read *Rolling Stone* and was thus very anti-establishment. I read *Private Eye* and was thus anti everything and everyone. I was anti!

And I stayed anti. For years on end, in my reviews and columns, I criticised everybody – judged them, ridiculed them, and laughed at them. I was fired as a film critic because I had let off steam against a respectable arthouse filmmaker. I was dragged before a judge because I had offended an experimental artist. I was angry! No – I was excessively angry. I was nothing but angry. I was always angry!

I had, because I had never been angry in my youth, built up a gigantic rage.

Then you are so dyspeptic and full of venom that you suddenly become angry at the wrong time, in the wrong place and with the wrong people. You become an irritable, bitchy, short-tempered, and poisonous person. You react with excessive anger to any people and situations that you can be angry about, often out of cowardice. You express your pent-up anger when you're safely in your car, you let off steam at your loving partner, and at the paper you're writing on. Or at weak people, such as children, insubordinates, check-out staff, animals, yourself, people on their own (if you're not on your own), foreigners, and so on.

I could have continued my life of anger for years – decades – without it making any difference, without anybody being so affected by my anger that he changed his life, and especially: without ever feeling satisfied myself.

There is only one way that I can put my puberty full of fury behind me. I must return to my old anger, the anger I never expressed, and try to resolve it. That means I have to examine the pain of my youth, the pain of rejection and being laughed at, the pain of feeling lonely and desperate, and the pain of never speaking up.

Let me stop with the exaggerated anger and taking revenge on people who have never done anything to hurt me.

TIPS

- What unexpressed pain, sorrow, frustration or fear is behind your anger? Examine it, feel it, and write it down. Accept the emotions in yourself, also the people in the situation at the time. Be sad and cry. What helps: watching a sad film and having a good cry.
- If you are always angry at A, you should realise that you may actually be angry at B. Is it a repetition of something from the past? And if you are thinking about B, is there perhaps some anger behind this at something or somebody else? Are you, perhaps, really angry with yourself?
- Even if you don't know why you are angry, if you know it is unjustified, just stop it. Act as if you aren't angry.

2 FAILURE

"Yesterday a superstar, today a dried pea"

The image I had of myself in my youth was rather extreme and very capricious. In my fantasy I was a pop star or a famous writer. On a stage, I accepted an ovation. People looked at me and thought me wonderful. I felt very sure of myself and radiated happiness.

Yes, I was simply the best!

But five minutes later, I could once again think I was a total failure. If somebody didn't say hello, I was devastated. You see!? Everyone thinks I'm worthless. If I walked past a group of laughing colleagues, I would retreat into my shell. Of course, they were laughing at me. Even an angry glance from a stranger, such as an anonymous shop attendant or a bus driver, was sufficient. I was wearing the wrong clothes or riding on the wrong scooter. I was either too shy or too rude. No matter what, it was never right.

This is reasonably normal behaviour for somebody in their puberty, but I still exhibit it. One of the forms that my superiority complex has assumed is the belief that I am more intelligent than others. I am virtually the only person who understands something and the rest are stupid and crazy. And everybody is going to know about this too. Know how wonderful I am and how stupid they are. Listen carefully to what I say! I have a very sharp eye and an exceptionally good intellect.

If I am so much better than others, then it follows that they are inferior. So, if I am worried that they may be better, then I deny this by belittling their success or by criticising and ridiculing them. I am, after all, better!

But deep inside there is the gnawing fear that I am nothing. If I am alone after some adversity, I feel myself the size of a dried pea. I am scared of everybody and see myself as a total failure. My youth, work, relationship, appearance – even my holidays and adventures. I never succeed at anything.

I never understood how I could be so contradictory. How was it possible that one minute I thought I was wonderful and the next nothing? If I thought about it, I called it my poisonous mix of feelings of superiority and inferiority.

That was until I discovered that these were not two different or even contradictory things, but one and the same. Because I consider myself so inferior and so hate that feeling, I would dream about how superior I am. And in order to convince others (but especially myself) that I am really wonderful, I constantly have to prove, exaggerate, and shout about it. If I remonstrate, exaggerate, and shout loud enough, I will believe myself (= narcissism). Perhaps. But not for long: the slightest adversity or well-directed criticism, and I once again think I am nothing.

The truth, as nearly always, is somewhere in the middle. I am sometimes nothing and I am sometimes wonderful. But often I am just average.

TIPS

- Write down ten qualities you have and ten things you have achieved that you are proud of.
- Write down the names of ten people that you feel good with and ten things you enjoy doing.
- Think rationally about an angry glance, a misfortune, a rejection, or a feeling as if you are a failure. Write down the extent to which you are exaggerating: "I am exaggerating, because if I think hard about it I realise that..."

3 CRISIS

"Panic. Chaos. Tears."

Things have gone wrong so often in my life, but this time everything exploded. Panic. Chaos. Tears. A full-blown crisis. I wasn't sure of anything anymore – or rather, I was sure that I couldn't go on like this. I noticed that I did all sorts of things as a matter of course without really wanting to do them. For example, I played with conviction the role of self-sacrificing partner, ever-angry complainer and gossip, ideal son, cynical intellectual, poison-pen columnist, recalcitrant employee, and misunderstood genius.

I was so confused that all I could do was end my relationship, stop working, stop doing everything. In retrospect I understand that it was a pause during which to reflect on what I really wanted. What I hadn't expected was that this reflection would force me to come back to the painful, still unresolved wounds of my youth. I reflected on the constant problems that, as a result of these wounds, poisoned and sabotaged my life. Why did I play all those roles if I didn't really want to?

I think that playing the roles was a reaction to old pain and day-to-day issues. The pain and problems had one thing in common: I felt inferior, and I wanted, with those roles, to prove something – prove that I was valuable. After all, I sacrificed myself, was critical, intellectual, and perfect, and others were less, otherwise I wouldn't complain so much about them. I played the roles to brag, to please people, to make others think: François is kind, tough, and a genius! Although I exaggeratedly played these tiring roles to prove that I was valuable, I felt increasingly like a phoney and a fraud, which meant that I had to go on playing those roles in order to prove myself... and so on.

What I really had to do was resolve all that old misery, and when, after a long time, I had managed to create a certain order, I no longer felt attracted to those painful roles. For the first time, I felt less worthless and thus felt less need to prove myself.

I could finally, step by step, stop playing roles and start being myself.

Long before this crisis, I had received signals that I was not feeling good, that I was sabotaging things for myself, that I had not resolved the old pain. But I overlooked all these signals because I was afraid of confronting all the misery and didn't feel like doing anything about it. We don't really like change.

You can avoid a major crisis by not avoiding small crises, by not denying but by accepting and doing something about the problems and pain in your life. If you ignore all the signals and thus avoid small crises, you won't avoid the major crisis: If you don't pay any attention to the pieces of gravel that hit your windscreen, you will be shocked when a brick comes through it. A major crisis means you are forced to stop avoiding things, and are given a chance to look at the problems and pain so that you can liberate yourself. A small crisis is a piece of gravel and less intrusive.

A crisis is a necessary evil.

TIPS

- What problems that you try to ignore have been there for years? What do you get signals about?
- Do you want to tackle a small crisis now or a major crisis in the future? Now you can choose the moment yourself; you won't be able to do that in the future.
- Take a look at one of the problems today, no matter how small, and do something to improve the situation... today!

4 COMPLAINING

"A good gossip"

I've spent a lot of my life complaining. I always have some criticism and rarely find things and people good enough to accept as they are. Generally, I find something to criticise about my neighbours, my friends, my partner, my baker, my work, my country, my family, and of course myself. I am unbelievably critical and that's extremely tiring.

But that's only the start of it because the worst thing is that I complain to A about B, and complain to B about A. I am always complaining about my partner to my friends. They must be sick to death of it by now. At home, I sit complaining about my colleagues so much that my partner can imitate their actions and words better than I can. I complain to my friends about my acquaintances and about my acquaintances to my cat. I never, ever complain to the person I'm complaining about.

All this became very clear to me one day when I sat complaining about people who do nothing else but complain. For Christ's sake, can't he stop nagging and whining? Why can't she stop going on about her husband and children to me? I can't do anything about it. But as always happens when somebody is complaining, I see myself sitting there patiently nodding and apparently agreeing with the person complaining and then, afterwards, I complain to somebody else that the person has been complaining to me.

If you complain to the wrong person – that is, not to the person that the complaint is about – the consequences are exclusively negative. You change nothing about what is actually wrong. If you complain to B about the behaviour of A, A will just continue happily doing the same thing, because he knows nothing about your displeasure. Secondly, you are wasting B's time, because he cannot change anything. As B listens, he will feel that he is being used and he will think (incorrectly) that he has to gossip along with you.

But the worst thing of all is that the person you are complaining about will eventually come to hear of it – indirectly. He hears that you have been complaining about him and the criticism will have been further exaggerated by the intermediary person – or worse, persons – and will thus hit home harder. The person you've complained about will feel hurt, the atmosphere will become charged, and what's more he won't feel at all motivated to change his behaviour – quite the contrary.

I am terribly scared and cowardly. I complain to the wrong person because I am scared that the person I am criticising will do something terrible to me if I complain to him or her in person. If I complain like that, then an argument always automatically follows. That's because if I complain personally to somebody once in a year, I've bottled things up for so long that I explode, and things escalate into a vulgar shouting match.

The solution is to complain to the person concerned but in a nice way, so that the person doesn't feel hurt and can move on with his or her head held high. It is better not to say: "Just stop doing things in this way!" and rather: "Would you please try to do this differently in the future?" And it's better not to say: "You do that wrong" but: "This is how it makes me feel." And finally, it is better not to wait too long, otherwise the wound will turn septic and start to stink.

It's healthy to complain, but you have to do it properly.

TIPS

- Only complain to the person who is the reason for the complaint.
- Say how it makes you feel.
- Frame the complaint with a request for something in the future.

5 SCARED

"Me, scared? Don't be silly"

There are a whole lot of things that make me scared. I'm scared of being deprived. I'm scared people will laugh at me, reject me, and that I will feel excluded. I'm scared of criticism – and scared that the criticism is justified! I'm scared that I haven't yet met my Great Love and never will. I would so like to be successful just once in my life in my work, stand on a stage and receive an ovation. But I'm scared that I am too old and not good enough. That can cause me to suddenly break into a sweat. Others are successful but I'm not. It all boils down to one thing: I'm scared that I'm worthless.

There is a certain type of person that I am immediately scared of: authoritarian, assertive, bossy people who act as if they are superior and who often hold positions of power. I immediately feel like a nice little boy when I meet them and I act like that as well. I become overly polite, start sucking up, and desperately try to please them. Please may I be one of you? I want their approval, because only then will I feel like I'm worth something.

Of course, I never get that pat on the back. Strong people have no compassion for weaklings who act like doormats. Quite the opposite: they only have respect for people who speak their language: dominant, authoritarian, implacable. Those beneath them get a kick in the butt. Want to belong? Bugger off!

The thing I am afraid of always happens. Because you are scared you act awkwardly and become irritated (angry at yourself because of your fear and insipid niceness), and in that way you create in others the very thing you are scared of.

It is just like my fear of being excluded, or my desire to belong. I am so scared that I will not be admitted to "that important clique" that I expect not to be admitted, and thus I am in advance furious about the fact that I am going to be rejected. And so, often without using words, I 'say': "Oh well, you won't think much of me and will reject me." And this has the predictable effect: "Oh, he doesn't think much of himself, and he knows best." Or: "Well, isn't that boy nervous, awkward, and irritated. Let's not include him." Or: "Boy oh boy, he really wants to belong – what's wrong with him?" C.S. Lewis wrote about wanting to belong: "Until you conquer the fear of being an outsider, an outsider you will remain."

You have to drag your fear out of its dark corner in order to get to know it. That means you have to complete your fear-ridden sentences. If I am not admitted, then… I won't die and, if I do my best, I'll find something else, no, perhaps even something better. If I don't receive an ovation, then I'll just have to do without like most people. And I can live with that.

If you want to overcome your fear, the one thing you mustn't do is run away from it, but, strange as it may seem, actually approach it, examine it, and especially: feel the fear. It's not that one person gets scared and the other doesn't. We are all scared. But one acts in spite of his fear, the other doesn't. The first is the result of a decision; the second happens automatically.

TIPS

- What scares you the most? Think what the very worst thing is that can happen. Imagine yourself in that situation. Will you die from all that misery or do everything possible to come out on top? What tangible things could you do?
- Write down at length what you are scared of; do not forget anything. Does this rhyme with reality? You're not exaggerating? Come up with three reasons why this is not based on reality.
- If the fear is realistic, do not avoid it and do not rest until there is a solution.

6 SILENCE

"Busy, busy, busy!"

Even when I'm sitting on the toilet, I examine the contents of my pockets to prevent myself from getting bored. I love having a lot to do, a packed diary, phoning everybody everywhere on their mobiles, having people around me, working hard, going off on holiday the whole time, and I love being busy, busy, busy. Of course, I complain about the never-ending rush and that I never have time for myself. But if I suddenly had nothing to do, then I would really start complaining. And time for myself? That would really put the cat among the pigeons.

What I really mean is: I avoid silence because I'm scared stiff of it. I'm scared of boredom (that's what I call it), scared of not having a full diary, of empty days, of loneliness, scared of going on holiday and not having anything to do, scared of an empty house and scared of silences if I am with anybody. I'm scared of any minute in which I don't have something to do and am always looking for noise. I deny it, but I'm really addicted to it.

What is behind my fear of silence? Behind it is my fear that through silence I will be confronted with myself, the fear that I will discover something that I have tried everything possible to avoid, the fear of having to spend time with my pain and sorrow, fear that I cannot handle that and that I may have to do something about the pain.

It seems as if the whole world is occupied every single day with searching for a new diversion so as not to have to feel the pain inside. Everybody is bungee-jumping, going on holiday five times a year, eating and drinking until they burst, buying expensive cars and boats; everybody is redecorating their houses and saying yes to everything and everybody. People are addicted to watching TV, chatting, going out, amusements, drugs, work, relationships, appearances, sex, complaining, alcohol, shopping, receiving applause, status, fame, winning, and other noise. Addicted to any form of anaesthetic – against the pain.

The world as it is now thinks it more normal that you are occupied with these diversions than if you don't allow yourself to be diverted and do what is important: sitting alone at home and coming to terms with yourself. Of course you have to eat, make love, earn money, and have fun, but why so addictively, so obsessively, so single-mindedly? Well, you exaggerate because then that diversion demands so much time and energy, and produces so much noise, that it rises above the voice of your own sorrow. When you're para-gliding, you can't worry about the pain from your youth. If you are a workaholic, there's not a moment left in the day to be sad about your relationship. If you are channel surfing, you can't wonder why you are neglecting your greatest dream.

What is so annoying and at the same time wonderful is that if you avoid your pain, it won't avoid you and will constantly and insidiously bother you, no matter how busy you make your life. If you examine your pain, if you listen to your sorrow, it will get better.

TIPS

- If you are always busy, you should look at what you are running away from. For that, you have to create silence.
- Once you have discovered the evil-doer, you must think about it, write it down, read about it, and talk about it. You will notice that you go through a variety of stages. Let that happen.
- If you get the feeling that you are bogged down, stuck, can progress no further, then go and talk to a therapist.

7 RESPONSIBILITY

"I can't do anything about that"

I used to think that the problem I had with responsibility was not accepting too little, but taking on too much. I ridiculed people who, after they had passed twenty, were still hoping that somebody would come along and rescue them, parents who wanted attention from their children instead of the reverse, and people who lived on benefits for years on end. I considered myself better than these so-called victims who avoided their responsibilities. I didn't only feel responsible for myself, but also for people in my circle, and I checked to see whether they were doing what they should be doing. I was even responsible for all the misery in the world.

This arrogant patina was scratched when I noticed that I often didn't feel responsible for things that were perhaps my responsibility. If I felt bad at work, I started complaining and gossiping. If I felt bad in my relationship, I became withdrawn and wallowed in self-pity.

I tried to kick against the pricks but slowly the truth dawned on me. I am responsible for the job and the relationship that I choose, and the state of my job and relationship. I am responsible for how much money I (don't) have, for my sex life, and for how fat I am. For the fact that I feel stupid, ugly, and a failure, and that most of my dreams have not come true. I am responsible for the way I look at my youth and what I do with it. You are one hundred percent responsible for your reaction in any situation. If you end up in prison, you are responsible for the way you deal with that.

There were other areas in which I acted irresponsibly, even childishly and helplessly. One day I felt like this, and the next like that, and that depended on a whole lot of circumstances, whether I was enjoying my work or had had a fight at home. The slightest thing knocked me off balance. But I never considered that it was possible to be responsible for how you feel.

You *are* responsible for how you feel. You no longer have to wind yourself up over things that have made you angry for twenty odd years. You don't have to be offended by things that have offended you until now. And you no longer have to let your mood be dependent on everything and everyone.

I am responsible for everything that I can change, so also the way I consider myself, undermine myself, and for my changing moods.

That came to me like a flash of lightning on a pitch-black country night. You don't have to wait, to complain, and to think: I can't do anything about it. The good news is: You can do something about it. And the bad news is: You can do something about it. It was wonderful knowing that I could change if I wanted to. And I did want to change.

I am responsible for my own (un)happiness.

TIPS

- Is there something you don't like that can be changed? (You can't change your past, your age, or the behaviour of other people.) For example: I want to be less negative.
- Write a page about it: why you do it, how you do it, when you do it, for how long you've done it, how it influences your life, what you are trying to avoid, and so on.
- Make a plan: what you want to have achieved in three weeks, three months, and three years, and what steps you have to take from today onwards. Be specific, for example: Every day I am going to tell myself something positive about myself and everyday I am going to tell somebody else something positive about him / her. In the evening, write down what you did.

8 SELF-PITY

"Poor little me!"

If somebody wasn't nice to me, I became withdrawn and started to sulk. "Poor little me!" Why me? Something like this only ever happens to me. How can I ever be happy? Everybody abandons me. Everybody else is doing great, everybody else has it easy, but for me it's always bad and difficult.

I could spend days going over the smallest little remark in my head. I always felt deeply hurt and unfairly treated. And then I began to wallow in self-pity: Look at all this pain I'm going through because of their horrible behaviour. You are all so mean! I'll show you just how unhappy you've made me. When somebody tried to comfort me, I became defiant: they'd hurt me and I could punish them by blocking their attempts to comfort me. My petty self-pity was greater than my desire to be comforted.

And that is sometimes still true. If, for example, I am not invited to a party and thus feel offended, I will do everything possible to avoid accepting an invitation that I receive "too late". I'll teach them. (Sob.) My partner's horrible, just like those people at work, my relations and the tax man. My whole life sucks. It's not fair. It's your fault!

My self-pity reasons like this: If I've been hurt, others have to ask me kindly what's the matter and after I've reacted huffily a few times ("mmm", "nooo", "bah!"), they have to persist and give me a lot of warmth and affection. Then perhaps – just perhaps – I can reward them by treating them normally.

Self-pity is a self-dug pit that I love to fall into. It is familiar and wonderfully lazy; you are the obvious victim and the others the perpetrators. It is a beckoning devil that I can still only resist with considerable effort. It's a perverse pleasure: it seems so wonderful, but it is so painful. It is painful because the so-called bad treatment makes you feel awful. What's more, from that moment on you are dependent on others; they have to pull you out of the pit and if they don't do that, you keep on feeling awful. Finally, it's painful because with such childish behaviour you chase away every reasonable person around you.

It was difficult for me to put an end to this because I am one of the many men (straight and gay) for whom self-pity is an important characteristic. I easily consider myself offended, hurt, and injured. I am wronged because I have been treated unfairly. That self-pity makes me yearn for attention, time, warmth, support, a helping hand ... from another person. Which, in this unpleasant way, I of course don't get.

I want others to comfort me, but I have to comfort myself. Men want Mother Mary, mummy, their wife / partner or girlfriend (and even their daughter) to comfort them, but you have to become your own mummy.

(Just as women have to become their own assertive daddy.)

Funnily enough, that makes it more attractive for others to comfort you and easier for you to accept it.

TIPS

- Behind self-pity lurks pain and repressed anger. Does it remind you of something from the past? Feel these emotions, listen to them, and try to write them down as fully as possible.
- Look at all the good things in your life, all the successes and highlights. Be grateful. Realise that you have arrived and have everything you ever wanted and are everything you ever wanted. (Only then can you get more.)
- You are not a dependent child, but an adult who knows that he is his own master. Analyse why you feel hurt and ask yourself whether that is justified. Was the insult intentional? Was it intended personally? Do people know that you are hurt? Are you squeaky clean? Do you have any right at all to what you want but didn't get? And do you have the right for somebody else to give it to you? Did somebody try to meet you half way, but you refused? Is it time to forgive somebody?

9 TO CONDEMN

"Ridiculing people is amusing"

To condemn is second nature to me; it is a great talent and I am extremely good at it. I seize every opportunity to criticise and ridicule people. My neighbours, my friends, my colleagues, my partner, and even myself – everyone! "Just look at that arse!" "Christ, she obviously got her driving licence at the drugstore!" "That TV show excels in stupidity!"

Not a minute passes without me condemning somebody or something. I once tried to stop for five minutes, but no matter what I thought or said, I couldn't even though I really tried my best. To judge isn't second nature to me – it's my first nature. I judge people, but they judge me too. Every condemnation hurts because I fear they are actually right. I don't enjoy criticism, but I cannot trust and respect people who do not condemn me.

I used to think: In this world, everybody condemns everybody else.

No – there is no such thing as *the* world; there are as many worlds as there are people. It is true that there is only one Mozart, but some like his music and others do not. Some are happy when the sun is shining, others are not. It's not about Mozart or the sun; it's all about how you look at things. Everything in your life passes through your own sieve. You see everything and everybody through your own glasses (sunglasses or rose-coloured spectacles): you can see mainly the bad things or mainly the good.

If I look through my sunglasses, I concentrate on the bad things. The bad things in this world, in people, and also in myself. Condemning others is the same as condemning yourself. When I meet new people, my brain rattles into action to come up with reasons why they are worthless. And I only remember what I don't like about people and what people don't like about me. That's the way I grew up. My parents criticised anybody who came to visit, preferably after they had left. At school, my friends and I criticised everybody we knew. My favourite books and magazines condemned everybody and everyone. I criticised my partner to my friends. I used to play the same game with my partner: together, we never thought anybody was good enough.

Now I know that criticising everybody has one cause: that you think that you yourself are a prick. And so everybody has to be brought down to your level so that you aren't the only prick around. And so I look for reasons why somebody isn't good enough and then I have the evidence that he's a prick. Simple. Seek and ye shall find. Journalism is a wonderful profession. Some comedians, columnists, and TV shows do nothing but condemn others.

If it's true that you create your own world, may I please live in a different one? I am sick to death of the world in which everybody, including myself, is a prick. In this self-made world, in which everybody condemns everybody else, you see, approach and explain everything in this light. Even well-meaning people become malicious enemies.

I am going to condemn something just one more time: the seemingly macho but really deeply hurt view of a world that condemns everything and everybody. Stop all this condemnation and start accepting and complimenting, and the world, your world will change radically.

TIPS

- Write down fifty things for which you are grateful: your body, the weather, your brains, your friends, and so on.
- Write down twenty names and after each one, write down a compliment that you could pay to him or her.
- Write down twenty things in your character that are good and twenty things that you have done well.

10 COMPLIMENT

"Stop sucking up!"

In the past, everything that smacked of a compliment was a problem for me. Paying a compliment was a problem. And receiving a compliment as well. It wasn't done to pay compliments. It was fine to criticise, because criticism was hip and proof that you were intelligent. But thinking something was good and actually telling the person concerned – that wasn't done. If you thought what somebody else had done was good, that meant – or at least, that's the way it felt – that you were placing yourself on a lower level to the person you were complimenting. Just the idea made me feel inferior, empty. Paying somebody a compliment felt like giving something away that then belonged to the other person. After the compliment, they were better, richer, and I was worse off.

When I was manager of a magazine and had to assess articles, I preferred not to react at all. The article appeared in print, or not, that was sufficient. If somebody nevertheless pressed me for a reaction, I'd beat about the bush. In the same period, I was also writing film reviews for a newspaper and nobody ever paid me any compliments. In the corridors of the newspaper colleagues told me that you only heard anything if something was wrong. By the way – that's how you had to review films for this newspaper: you only told people what was wrong with a film.

If you think of compliments in this light, life becomes one long race. A race you can win or lose. And if you're not winning, then you're losing. And then you're pathetic, a loser. In this vision, everybody has a sort of status report showing all victories and defeats. If you receive a compliment, you move up the list and if you give a compliment, you move down. If you have a low place in the pecking order – or think you do – then you certainly wouldn't want to drop any further by giving somebody a compliment so that he or she moves up a place or two. The more you consider yourself a loser, the more difficult it becomes to pay a compliment.

You would think that if you consider yourself a loser, then it must be wonderful to receive a compliment. Quite the opposite: if you think you are a loser, you can't believe compliments and simply throw them into the bin.

When I started feeling better about myself and wanted to be done with all this nonsense, I asked myself two questions: OK – but when are you going to pay a compliment? And second: How are you going to accept a compliment? I had so little experience with either and felt so paralysed by the idea that I simply didn't know what to do. The answer to the second question is: You say "Thank you." The answer to the first question is: when you think somebody has done something good or noteworthy.

If I now get a compliment, I know when I can believe it. If I pay somebody a compliment, I notice that I do not feel worse for it but better. You know that it is honest and that makes you feel better.

Somebody has done something good, so why should you remain silent about it? And the person who receives the compliment also feels better. Everybody feels better.

After giving and receiving compliments became normal, suddenly giving and receiving criticism became easier.

TIPS

- If somebody pays you a compliment, always say thank you. If you later begin to doubt it, think as rationally as possible about whether your doubt is justified.
- If somebody does something good then pay a compliment. Do you feel better or worse?
- Did you in the past ever forget to pay a compliment? Did you ever forget to say thank you when you were paid a compliment? Do it now.

11 HARMONY

"Harmony often seems fake"

I've always been mad about harmony. I want everything to be calm, take a lot of trouble to achieve it, and adapt radically if that proves necessary. If I can pay the price to avoid discord, I do that automatically. I'm proud that I don't argue, that I'm from a family that didn't argue, and, to be quite honest, I rather look down on people who quarrel. Particularly if they start shouting. And absolutely if there are others present. Of course, I have my differences of opinion (that's my way of putting it), but these are discussed without raised voices and in privacy. And if I am really honest, preferably not discussed at all.

I have always had a vague suspicion that there is something not quite right with my harmony. It always fell flat. The harmony was always at the expense of myself and at the expense of other people and things.

That vague suspicion has changed into a strong conviction, ever since I came to understand that there is a difference between what I call fake harmony and real harmony. Yes, there are two types.

Fake harmony means that nobody says what he or she really thinks; we pretend we agree on everything about which we disagree. Everybody runs around wearing a mask with a bright smile painted on it. This lack of communication results in misunderstandings, loss of time, gossip, stomach aches and chaos. Behind the neat facade of silence and false smiles there lurks considerable repressed anger. I have always sought and achieved this fake harmony.

Perhaps I was simply too addicted to harmony. I am scared of conflicts and virtually everything that involves saying out loud in somebody's presence what you really think, defending yourself, and quarreling, and thus feeling uncomfortable and scared. And yet I have discovered that it is better to tell each other the truth than to walk around with a stomach ache. In fact, I believe that telling each other the truth – and that often leads to conflict and quite the reverse of harmony – is necessary to achieve true harmony. True harmony is a must if you want to work together, really work together: so that you achieve with as many colleagues as much as possible in the shortest possible time. You can call it enthusiasm or flow.

It is, as so often is the case, a matter of choosing between two evils: do you want a short-term or a long-term solution? The first solution is no solution. People are, in principle, never immediately in complete agreement with each other. If differences of opinion are not discussed, not resolved, you end up with a stomach ache and other assorted misery. If you do discuss it, you may, it is true, quickly find yourself in a conflict, but that is often followed by clarity and even a feeling of unity. Even a conflict that results in an eternal divorce (of minds) is progress, albeit very small. Otherwise you'll continue secretly sabotaging each other with half truths, smoke and mirrors, and gossip.

I don't aim for real harmony with everybody, just with those people that I deal with a lot, such as friends, family, and colleagues. Otherwise, fake harmony (=politeness) is often sufficient.

This chapter does not only apply to friends and colleagues, but especially to romantic relationships, even the one you have with yourself. Quarrel!

TIPS

- If you find harmony, do you feel harmonious?
- Are you scared of conflict? Feel the fear and do it just the same! (Samuel Johnson said: "The less we quarrel the more we hate.")
- How to complain? You'll find the best way to do that in the chapter on "Complaining".

12 SUCCESS

"I've got to be a success!"

There was a time when I had exciting work, plus a certain reputation, and to top it all of, earned a lot of money. Yet I was dissatisfied, irritated, and had physical problems. I chased after every goal that would have brought me success, and I achieved those goals with considerable effort and damage. But I was not happy. Had I chased the wrong goals? Had I forgotten others?

Working in tv I have known many celebrities: tonnes of money, status ("I am important, hip, and sincere") and as famous as can be. But their private lives were a mess and they were destroying their minds and bodies. They wore an iron mask, but they had no idea of what was behind the mask because they denied it with all their might. You can wear expensive suits, live in an impressive house, and drive around in a "look at me now" car, but that only makes things worse, because the comparison with your sorry private life becomes so alarmingly black and white.

Think about somebody who is rich, important, famous and dissatisfied with their life. And think about somebody who is poor, unimportant, unknown and satisfied with their life. Who is successful?

I had never seriously asked myself what I meant by success, what it meant to me. And what failure meant to me. I had started the race without knowing whether perhaps I should be participating in a different race altogether.

That different race didn't mean immediately starting running, but first allowing yourself to get to know who you are, what you like, what your talents and dreams may be, how hard you want to work, and how much money you wish to earn. But true success is also: What sort of person do I want to be, do I want to be employed or independent, honest or not, a workaholic or a good partner and parent? Finally, success is also: Do I want to get to know myself and then *be* myself? Because that's the only place you'll find peace and happiness.

Don't think I'm suggesting that you become a pauper or a hermit. Try to get to know who you really want to be and what you will want to do and try to earn as much money, respect, and fame through it as possible. Sometimes, the person you want to be will come into conflict with earning as much money as possible; try to find a balance by sometimes choosing one, and sometimes choosing the other.

There are many books focused on finding success. One of the things all these books say is that you must have goals. You should write these down and divide them into smaller units. You should ask others to help you, look at the way you work against yourself, and set deadlines. Then you have to do everything possible within your power to achieve your goals. This is simply a matter of common sense and it is good advice to follow. But choose the right goals and don't become tense and morose.

If you run the first race, the chance is considerable that even if you win, you lose. So, there is really no other choice: the only way to be really successful is to take part in the other race.

TIPS

- Write down what sort of person you want to be and what you would like to do with your life. What does success mean specifically for you?
- What would you like to achieve in three years in order to feel successful? Write down what is necessary if you are to achieve this.
- Write down your goals and don't stop until you have achieved them!

13 TENSE

"You can do it if you really really want to"

Everybody knows the stories from American movies: If you really want something and you really, really do your best, you'll succeed in the end! People who have become fabulously wealthy newspaper magnates were once paupers, but thanks to pure willpower, they succeeded in becoming incredibly successful.

A positive message like this always reignites in me a glowing aspiration. You see? If you really want to, if you really, really want to achieve something, then all you have to do is your very, very best. I have always wanted to become rich and famous and that desire has never left me. But I have never gone to every length, and, indeed, I'm still not rich and famous.

In general, we are lazy – at least, I am – and we think and dream that what we want will simply drop into our laps. Or at least, we will achieve our goals with the least amount of effort. Hard reality has shown me that both suppositions are illusions. So, in fact I agree completely with the optimistic message from those American films.

But still, at a certain moment I noticed that, at the same time, this message was false. The first time I noticed it was when I was in love and pursuing the person in question. The more I did my best, the worse the situation became. The same thing happened with a job application. I wanted that job so badly and did everything I could to get it. But the result was that I turned up far too early, became extremely nervous, and even began to suck up to people. I wanted it so badly. But I didn't get the job.

Another example: If, in a discussion, I really want to convince somebody that I am right, I know from the start that the other will dig his heels into the ground, and will either argue back or say nothing and secretly label me a plonker.

I think this is where it goes wrong. People become distrustful if I want something so desperately. Can't he get a partner, job, or agreement in a normal way? Even more importantly, people are quite willing to give you their friendship, a job, or agree that you are right, but it has to be "giving". If you really want something, it's almost as if you are stealing it from them and they can no longer give it. People think you're greedy and egocentric, feel themselves manipulated and don't like that feeling one little bit. If you nevertheless continue nagging after they've said no, the other person does not feel respected – and rightly so. You never give these people the chance to think: I don't only think it's nice to give, it's also in my interests to do it.

You can therefore go too far with your enthusiasm. It's necessary, but you have to adopt a certain suppleness, as if you are playing. Not too serious, not too nervous.

If you want something, you mustn't want it too much.

TIPS

- Don't just sit there quietly waiting, but say clearly what you want and why. Then leave the other person in peace to decide what he or she wants to do. Never force anybody!
- If you don't get what you want, say that you regret it but realise there is nothing to do about it.
- If you get a "no" and still want it, don't keep ringing the same doorbell; look for a new one. There's a good chance that sooner or later you'll get what you want. Don't give up.

14 PERFECT

"I prefer not to make mistakes"

I remember somebody once telling me that it was quite alright for me to make mistakes. I immediately got goose pimples, and an enormous wave washed over me, a wave screaming out "NO!". Make mistakes? Me? Why would I do that? I prefer not to make mistakes. Or better still: I don't make mistakes.

Anybody who doesn't make mistakes must, for everything that goes wrong – and things go wrong all the time in everybody's life – find a guilty party other than themselves. I placed the blame for everything that went wrong in my work on my colleagues and, in particular, on my boss. I placed the blame for everything that went wrong in my relationship on my partner. If I had any issues, about no matter what, the other person had caused them. I didn't make mistakes; I was apparently perfect. If you had said that to me, I would have put on a supposedly modest smile and said: "Well, of course I'm not perfect ..." But if you had then pressed me on what I had actually done wrong, you would have got a silly or irritable answer.

This arrangement I had with the world – that it was always the other person that was guilty and never me – didn't work. The other person didn't think it fair. But I simply kept on repeating that he – and not me – was the reason for everything that went wrong. That caused a lot of misery. And I blamed the other person for that as well. Didn't he realise he was wrong?

I could have gone on like this for ever. A life full of conflicts that were always the responsibility of other people. Until I finally saw through this mechanism. Apparently, I found it necessary to show the world a mask of perfection. And I needed that mask because I was afraid that people would be able to see what really lurked behind that mask: a yellow-belly who was always petrified that he would actually make a mistake. I had to deny this possibility as vociferously as possible and thus I wore the mask of somebody who never makes a mistake. Apparently, making mistakes was taboo. (A narcissist adores his perfect mask / image and hates the vulnerable, sorry truth behind it.)

When I slowly began to admit my faults (extremely difficult!) and accepted responsibility for them, my life became a lot nicer. I saw that I could put my mistakes right and get more power over my life. I no longer quarreled with myself when I looked in the mirror after cleaning my teeth and took off my mask. I no longer heard that little voice saying to me: "You idiot, you were wrong there, and now you're placing the blame on the other person."

My life is now a lot calmer. If I make a mistake, I try to acknowledge it. If, after reasonable reflection, I think the other person is to blame, I am satisfied that I have reached that decision. If somebody then disagrees with that, I simply shrug. I know I have been reasonable and know that, if it were necessary, I would have taken the blame myself. I don't really need the other person to say that I am right.

I still find it very difficult to admit to mistakes, but I do it more and more and my life is a lot easier.

TIPS

- Do something that you enjoy but are not good at, and have therefore neglected trying. Say to yourself: I am allowed to make all the mistakes in the world.
- Set aside one day and use it to do nothing important, useful, or whatever you usually do. Spend a whole day relaxing with simple things, such as playing with your children.
- If somebody else makes a mistake, accept that lightheartedly and make that clear to the other person.

15 LOVE

"Love is a beautiful, deep feeling"

What did I think in my youth when I heard or read the word "love"? One thing I know for certain is that I never used it myself – much too scary. I understood that the word was used in different ways by all sorts of people. Love in a pop song was something different to what my parents shared or what some people called the love of God.

I didn't really attach much importance to love. It was just one of those things that would come in time. And when those things did come, I naturally assumed I had been right all along. Love was something that people had when they loved each other. Yes, but what was it? A very beautiful and deep feeling, that's what it was!

When I fell in love and suddenly felt that very beautiful and deep feeling for somebody, that was love. Now I loved somebody. And if the other person was also in love with me, that was real true love.

When you first fell in love, you had a very intense, feverish feeling. But that passed. Then suddenly you felt those beautiful, deep feelings for each other less frequently. If those beautiful feelings were absent for long enough and the empty place was filled with feelings of anger and disappointment, then there was no love left. Then you split up. I sometimes felt powerless about the way things went, but that's just the way life was.

Until I started reading authors such as Erich Fromm and M. Scott Peck and things slowly began to dawn on me. Thinking that love is a beautiful and deep feeling is now for me comparable to thinking that the earth is flat. The earth is round. And love has nothing to do with emotions. Well, a little, of course; it often starts with falling in love but that turns, if things go well, into love. And this brings us to what I discovered: with the phrase "if things go well" in the previous sentence I mean: if you want it and if you do it. Love is thus something that you must want and then something that you must do. It doesn't happen spontaneously and is not dependent on all sorts of feelings.

After a while I reached the conclusion that it often comes down to two tangible things: time and attention. If you give the other your time and attention, then you love the other, you give the other love. And what you must want and then do with that time and attention is make the other happier with it. Another person will not be happier because of your deep feelings. Another person can become happier thanks to the things you say or do.

Another person will not be happier if you hit him or lie to him. Another person will be happier if you are kind to him. But another person will also be happier if you are honest with him. And often honesty can be awkward, for you but especially for the other person. How can somebody be happier if you do or say something awkward? It is awkward in the short term, but in the long term it is actually good. For example, if you say: please, stop lying.

Something similar is: not saying or not doing something that you like, giving something up, so that the other person is happier for it. For example, by saying no to a child demanding an ice cream, no matter how convenient it would be to say yes.

Sometimes love can be downright awkward.

TIPS

- If you love somebody, say or do things that help make that person happier, healthier, and more mature as a person.
- Stop saying or doing things that make somebody less happy, less healthy, and less mature as a person.
- Do things without wanting something in return, so without the other loving you in return.

16 CYNICAL

"Everything and everybody is crap"

More than ten years after the Second World War, I grew up in Holland thinking that the world and the people in it were fundamentally bad. The authors I read preached a nihilistic image of the world and my heroes were cynical columnists.

Cynicism means thinking people and the world are bad. I understood why my favorite authors were so angry and depressed. Wars, concentration camps, torture, famine, stupidity, hypocrisy, treachery, and deceit – these were all things that people did to each other. In my puberty, I completely agreed with the authors I read. Cynicism was macho and I became a grumpy, complaining sourpuss.

Everybody knows those sickly American tv series in which daddy happily does chores with his son and mummy hums sweetly as she bakes cookies with her darling daughter. Life is so wonderful and fine! Born again Christians who have found Jesus show that same manic and artificial happiness. I'm so happy that I'm so happy, Hallelujah! It gives you the creeps. This way of looking at reality is called sentimental. It is an over-the-top way of looking at life, and just as much a lie as the opposite, cynical view. The creeps are caused by the lies. Describing life as exclusively good or exclusively evil is wrong in either case.

It is easy and says much about you and little about reality. You are lazy; you don't have to bother thinking. Whatever happens, you persist in finding life either wonderful or disastrous. If you think that life is exclusively wonderful/disastrous you intentionally close your eyes to all ugly/beautiful things. It is more difficult and much braver to have to decide for every person and in every situation whether they are good or bad or something in between. And honestly admit this. Otherwise you reduce the gigantic, colourful, blinding reality to a simplistic black and white caricature.

Cynicism may seem macho and hip, but it is dangerous; it poisoned much of the first half of my life. If you think the world is only dirty and evil, you live in that world. (Because an objective world does not exist; everybody lives in the world they create for themselves.) And then you also see yourself as nothing but dirty and evil. If you severely condemn the world, you severely condemn yourself. If you look at the world with optimism, compassion, and forgiveness, you look at yourself in the same way.

It took me considerable time and effort to understand that people and life can, at the same time, be wonderful and rotten. It is not either / or but and / and. Life and people are horrible and wonderful, delightful and painful, revolting and delicious. And all 98 shades of grey in-between. And I am as well. I am terribly bad, but also terribly good, but mainly all those shades of grey.

Cynicism may seem exciting and original and shades of grey may seem boring and predictable. But isn't thinking that everything /

everybody is either bad or beautiful exactly that: dull and predictable?

TIPS

- Describe ten situations in which your cynical attitude has poisoned your life. Examples: Your work, your relationship, your friends, the type of parent you are, the way you spend your spare time, how you think of yourself.
- How do you profit by looking at the world as only evil? Do you want to belong to the trendy intelligentsia that think in that way? Are you lazy and do you not want to think for yourself? Why are you afraid of thinking positive thoughts?
- Put a clock on the table and try, either alone or with one or more other people, to spend ten minutes thinking of all the good things rather than the bad things in the wide world around you and the small world inside you. Write them down.

17 FAIR

"The world must become better"

I used to read the paper every day and watch without fail the eight o'clock news. I saw bleeding bodies on the street, bodies that had been wounded by yet another bomb. I heard about earthquakes and floods that made thousands of innocent people homeless. I read about parents who had raped or murdered their children. And every day I was astonished again by all this misery. I had a pitch-black view of the world, but I was nevertheless angry and sad every day afresh.

If I really had such a dark view of the world, could I really have expected anything else? Apparently I thought that it should get better – no, that the world actually should already be honest and righteous. And as long as that wasn't the case, I remained angry and sad. And completely amazed.

Why isn't the world just? A thirty-year-old mother who led an honest life is knocked down and killed by a drunk driver and the head of a criminal organisation dies peacefully in his bed at the age of ninety. And 23 million other injustices in this world that take place every single day. I used to drive myself crazy with such thoughts. Even if the world became just starting tomorrow, it would never be good enough because of all the countless horrors that have taken place in the past.

I have worked for years in television and all those years I have looked with sadness and anger at the things offered by tv. There are modest, honest, and capable people working in television, but what do you see on the box? The Kardashians, Big Brother, and Jerry Springer.

It's the same everywhere. Our government is often unjust, wheel clamping is unjust, my boss is unjust and so is my partner. I think the world is unjust! And that the world has always been unjust. And that that will always be the case. Sometimes it gets worse, sometimes marginally better, but no matter what, it is pretty awful. I'll just have to accept that. Really accept it. The world is like that, people are like that, my parents are like that, my boss is like that, and so, too, is my partner. And I'm very often like that as well.

The strange thing is that when I really tried to accept this and let it penetrate to my very core, it seemed as if a burden had fallen from my shoulders. The burden of desiring and hoping and secretly expecting that it would become better, that it *must* become better. The burden of complaining and nagging. The burden of having to improve everything. The burden that in the meantime I had no right to enjoy myself.

I used to look on the world with anger and impotence, and in that way I could change nothing. It was all too bad and all too much. It made me angry. It paralysed me. When I read the paper in the past, I thought: Oh that's terrible! It will never turn out right anymore! When I read the paper now, I am more resigned and that gives me the peace to suggest small changes (yourself, your partner, your neighbours). Don't get angry, don't complain, don't expect anything, but, reasonably relaxed, make a small effort that may, perhaps, lead to an even smaller improvement. Concentrate on the drop, not the ocean.

Accept the injustice of the world and you can make it more just.

TIPS

- Think how often and for how many years you have thought something unjust. Has your worrying, complaining, and getting angry made anything even the slightest bit better?
- You first have to "accept" (acknowledge) a problem before you can change it.
- See what you can change, even to the most microscopic degree, in all that injustice.

18 VICIOUS

"Teasing is fun, don't you think?"

A friend once made me aware of how I sometimes acted when I met somebody for the first time. No matter how nice the other person was – or rather, exactly because they were so nice – I would at once start making small provocative remarks and subtle digs. Time and again, I would try to provoke people so that I could pounce on things they never had intended to say in the first place.

Of course, I denied this ("No – it wasn't as bad as that!") or justified it ("I was bored and made a few bad jokes"), but I knew better. Even after I had resolved to stop doing it, I continued to amaze myself by simply carrying on in the same way.

That friend thought it a particularly nasty habit because I myself am hypersensitive to criticism: if somebody makes a dig at me, I almost choke with rage. I am very easily wounded and at the same time I want to take a dig at everybody; in fact, cause them pain. I act like a venomous teenager. I want to get the better of everybody, but if you try something like that on me, I squeal like a stuck pig.

Why do I start bleeding at the slightest criticism, but continue hurting others, and what's more, enjoying it? The more I hurt somebody else, the more I gloat. Isn't that the definition of sadism? I am afraid that in the past I have been hurt too much and too often, without having hit back. If I now feel hurt (and that happens all too easily), all that past misery that has lain rotting and stinking surfaces and I react with an exaggerated forcefulness.

That I now have the chance to hit back almost makes me happy: Aha! Now I'm big and powerful! Now I'll really hit back! I enjoy it so much that I am only satisfied when the other person feels as crappy, hurt, and uncomfortable as I used to feel back then. You would think that because I know how that feels I would be more sensitive, but the reverse is true.

My weaponry includes snide remarks, sabotage, misuse of power, surly body language, and my style is venomous, uncharitable, and savage. I spread an atmosphere of discontent, fear, and conflict. Behind my back, people call me mean, bitter, and malicious. If it ever comes up in conversation, I play the victimised innocent and blame others.

Why have I developed the mechanism that I describe in the first paragraph? I am so scared that people will hurt me that I do not take any risks and get in the first blow: Don't you dare hurt me! I feel so vulnerable that I must immediately strike. Others have to be kept in their places. I am like an old dog that has been chained up and beaten so often that it trusts nobody and immediately starts growling and biting.

Being vicious is a mask for being hurt.

TIPS

- Stop hurting people.
- Tell all those people that you have terrorised for all those years that you are sorry and will never do it again. Ask them to warn you with a word or a sign if you start doing it again.
- Try to resolve those unhealed wounds from your youth, otherwise you will carry on surprising yourself with small explosions.

19 PAIN

"I don't want any pain today"

Sometimes I think that nobody has had to suffer so many secret humiliations as I have faced. In my youth I was invisible, as if I didn't exist. At school, I couldn't stop myself being invisible and was thus, apparently, not worth the bother. Worthless. I was nothing. When, even now, thirty years later, I think back to the bullying at school, tears of rage and frustration spring to my eyes. For ten years, my law studies were a prospectless agony of stomach aches, apathy, and self-hate.

I thus knew that pain existed. But did I really know that?

I once dined with a good friend during a desperate period in my life. I was drowning in my own misery. I spoke and he listened. After a dramatic pause, he sighed and said: "Well, François, pain's part of the deal." I was shocked by this cold remark. Didn't he like me anymore?

Or did he just want to stop my complaining? My food stuck in my throat.

No, he meant it. He wanted to comfort me: I wasn't the only person who felt pain, everybody had to face it at some time or another. And anyway, can you really enjoy life if you never suffer any pain? But wait a moment – I've known all this for ages! So why was I shocked? Had I forgotten?

We have all grown up with the idea, without anybody having told us in so many words, that life is worth living. That's why we get out of bed every morning. That our life is often difficult, hopeless, terrible, incredibly painful, and sometimes unbearable – that's something we aren't told. That's the way I grew up and there's something in me that says: Yes, life sometimes may be difficult, but difficult for others. But not for me! And not today! I don't want any pain today and if I do feel it, I will be deeply unhappy.

We should talk more about our pain, not about the train being delayed but about the fact that life leaves nobody untouched, and that all of us, even Bill Gates, the Pope and Beyoncé, regularly face sorrow, misery, degradation, and failure, and – yes – sometimes even unbearable pain.

We can arm ourselves not against the existence of pain, but against the way we deal with it. You can reduce the pain – not by denying it, but by talking about it, examining it, smelling it. Sometimes you just have to accept. Sometimes it is a signal to do something else. Sometimes it means you have to forgive somebody and let go of the pain. But we all get our share. Pain is part of the deal.

The more you deny pain or resist it, the more it rules your life. Once you accept that pain is part of the deal, your life becomes more bearable, less painful.

TIPS

- Do you argue about small things? Do you become irritated by insignificant matters? Do you react angrily to nothing? Then you are denying (something that causes) pain.
- You can only let go of pain after you have taken hold of it. So, search for it, take hold of it, smell it, and especially: accept that it is there.
- Realise that you are a human being and thus, by definition, you will have suffered pain, are suffering pain, and will suffer pain. Don't deny it and don't put it off, but look at it and talk, read, and write about it. A good cry also helps, but do something positive, don't get angry and bitter and don't go to bed with a stomach ache or clenched teeth.

20 SEX

"I want more and better sex"

I grew up in the sixties and seventies – during the sexual revolution. During my puberty in Holland I could buy porn anywhere without any problem. I was told that, unfortunately, sex used to be forbidden but happily that was no longer the case. Having sex, just like eating fruit, was marketed as a necessary prerequisite for a normal, healthy life.

When I entered a relationship, I automatically assumed that this would include a whole lot of sex. That was the case, but it soon grew less. We told each other that sexually we had grown a little tired of each other. I thought that the increasingly uninteresting sex was an important reason why, a little while later, we split up.

In my current relationship, that has now lasted for more than thirty years, I had, for a long time (at least ten years, I think) bad sex. I wanted this, he wanted that. I wanted it often, he didn't. I blamed him for this, he blamed me for that. Talking about it always resulted in an enormous argument, followed by a sexual arousal that didn't last longer than just one adequate sexual session.

Living in Amsterdam in the eighties and nineties gave me the feeling that everybody in the city were screwing themselves senseless. Except us. What's wrong with us? What's wrong with me? Doesn't he find me attractive anymore? I'll be honest. I often thought: What's wrong with him? Is he doing it with others?

Should we do different things, try some games, use some toys? There were times when I was desperate. (I didn't yet know that sex was more or less always a problem, for everybody, everywhere.)

In retrospect, I see that I was searching for a sexual solution to my sexual problem. I was sure: that sexual solution would make our relationship better again. If we had better sex, our relationship would once again become better.

I don't know how I discovered it, but I do know what I thought: Why didn't I discover this sooner? You see, the reverse is true. You can of course have exciting sex with a stranger, but in a relationship good sex is not the cause of a good relationship but the result. First there is a good relationship, and only then great sex. If you have too little or bad sex and you blame your partner your relationship deteriorates, and then the sex gets worse, and so on and so on; it's a vicious circle.

The reason that so many people in our society have a bad sexual relationship with their partner is not because there is something sexually wrong with them, but because their relationship is bad.

Sex is never just about sex.

TIPS

- Would you like more / better sex? Then make sure you have a better relationship.
- Do nice things for your partner without expecting anything in return.
- Talk about sex, be open about what you want, and be one hundred percent honest.

21 SPECIAL

"It's nice to stand out"

When, in the past, I wanted – no, demanded – something special, I said to myself that I was somebody who really enjoyed all sorts of things and that I therefore wanted to get the most out of life. Yes, I was strong-willed and obstinate. When I was still young I wanted long hair and hip clothes, because I had to stand out at school. When, at the age of twenty, I bought my first car, it simply had to be a sports car. I wanted to be special in comparison to my friends.

At a given moment, I started calling that obstinacy ambition. I was looking for an impressive job, a very attractive partner, a car that drew attention, regular exotic holidays, the nicest place to live, an unusual house, and more attention, status, and applause than others. I absolutely had to have all these things. I had to be the best, I had to be the centre of attention, I absolutely had to be special! I acted as if I had more right to this than others.

For years – I now realise in retrospect – I was preoccupied with being special and better than others in order to get the world's admiration. Admiration is something that others give you, so I had to make an impression on them so that they would give it to me. In fact, I manipulated others to give it to me.

One of the worst and at the same time most stubborn aspects of wanting to be special is that I wanted – no, needed – to be respected. People had to see me as somebody important, and I had to belong to the "right circle". So, then you want to belong to those people who "really matter" and you start making remarks that will most appeal to their taste. You start sucking up to the powerful, and so you become hypocritical, politically correct and overly willing to please. You arrange your whole life so that the world has to respect you. When I started to write, I could only come up with the most politically correct newspaper and, later, working on tv, only the most politically correct network. Please may I be one of you? Then I will say everything and do everything you desire of me! And so I sold my soul to the devil.

Unfortunately, it didn't work. If you want to be considered special, you're seen as a poseur and bragger. The more you wheedle for respect and do your best to get it, the more people think of you as a creep and a brown-noser. The more you want to be appreciated by others, the less likely you are to succeed.

The people who are respected and admired are those that don't look for respect and admiration. The more honest and independent you are – thus, the more yourself – the more you will get admiration and respect. If you tell people the truth, they may not like you but they will respect and admire you. If you don't tell people the truth but only say what they want to hear, they won't admire and respect you but think you are a frightened, weak nobody.

And that's also what you think of yourself. The more admiration and respect you seek, the more you apparently think yourself a loser and really need that applause – from others.

Admire and respect yourself, your real self, and the world will imitate that to the same degree.

TIPS

- If you respect yourself, you don't let people walk all over you and thus force others to respect you. If, for example, you respect your time and protect it with great care, you will teach others to do the same through remarks and ultimatums. And the reverse: if you don't respect your own time, you give off signals: treat my time carelessly and without respect, just as you see me doing, you won't hear any complaints from me.
- If you admire a characteristic in yourself, for example telling the truth, you will show by acting honestly that you are honest, and words will become unnecessary. People believe behaviour and – rightly – place less weight on words.
- Don't try to belong to the circle that is important and "really matters", but to the group that, in your field, does good, honest things.

22 ADULT

"Growing up is boring"

One of the things I now see clearly is that I remained an obedient child for so long. I was a mummy's boy that did everything expected of him. My parents were angry at my naughty brother and I wanted them to like me. So, I was obedient, industrious, polite, and hypocritical. By pleasing them, I got stuck in the role of the obedient child and was not myself.

It was only later that I exploded and became an angry, rebellious teenager. I was against everything and everybody related to authority, anybody who was the boss, anybody who was a substitute for my parents. After all those well-behaved years, I could finally take my pound of flesh. I rebelled against my parents, but mostly against my school and teachers, against the arrogant, hypocritical people in power, against the established order; I chose the side of the offended shouters.

I only felt good if others felt uncomfortable, because everybody had to feel just as bad as I did. My method was provoking, challenging, hurting, rebelling, and fighting against everything and everybody. I was thirty and still wanted to know just how far I could go. I kicked at sacred cows (that's the way I described things to justify my behaviour) and it wasn't without justification that people called me an *enfant terrible*. I rebelled in an outlandish fashion and was once again not myself.

Compared with the behaviour of an obedient child, the rebellious teenage behaviour seems exactly the opposite. Seems – because doing exactly the opposite is a different way of doing exactly the same. You do things simply to do the opposite. I was initially overly willing to please; later I was belligerent. Initially I placed my faith in conformism, later in non-conformism. Initially I was Cliff Richard, later Michael Moore. The calculated blandness of Cliff Richard is offensive, just as the calculated offensiveness of Michael Moore becomes bland in the long run.

After all my tantrums, it seemed a good idea to give up my role as rebellious teenager, but also that of an obedient child. Both roles were equally untruthful; each was a mask behind which I could hide. When I occasionally took off the mask, I realised that thinking and acting in set patterns was a point I had passed. I had to think things over, think for myself. Who was I? Was I docile? Or was I angry? When I thought something over, I noticed that I was sometimes for and sometimes against, but that I always chose a solution that seemed sensible and wise. In other words, I had finally, without knowing it, chosen to become an adult.

People with whom I acted like an obedient child, such as a friend I admired considerably, sometimes with my powerful boss and often with my strict mother, suddenly found to their surprise that I was no longer so amenable. I no longer immediately said yes.

Others with whom I acted like an angry teenager, such as with a friend who admired me considerably, sometimes with my authoritarian boss (!) and often with my kind father, suddenly found it remarkable that I was no longer so rebellious. I no longer immediately said no. It must have been confusing for some people to see me both pliable and insubmissive.

Growing up is working; you have to think things over, rely on your own judgement, no longer saying or doing something in order to elicit a certain reaction from others (that is manipulation and always happens because of fear) but because you really mean it. Slowly you become an autonomous, authentic, responsible person who thinks, feels, says, and does things because he has thought them up himself. I think that what people currently call personal growth is, for a large part, growing up. This sounds joyless, but the surprising reward is that growing up is the only way to become yourself and thus to experience authentic joy.

It was not until I reached forty that I tried to grow up.

TIPS

- Are there people with whom or situations in which you feel small, you easily say yes, and later think: I'm acting like a doormat?
- Are there people with whom or situations in which you feel big, better than the other person, in which you do not take the other person seriously and later think: why did I act so imperiously?
- Why do you act in this way? What fear are you trying to avoid? How could you behave differently?

23 HAPPY

"Happy? Sure – ten seconds a year"

I have often felt bad in my life. I hated bad weather, so if it was cold or raining, I became irritable. If I was disappointed by the food in a restaurant I became sour: You go to a restaurant, pay good money, and then you're served this rubbish! When I read the paper I became angry at all the misery I found there: greedy businessmen, corrupt leaders, parents who abused their children, and a literary prize for the next snobbish author. Has everybody gone crazy?!

My work never fully satisfied me. I was in the wrong place and had to walk on eggshells or crawl. I almost always had problems with whoever was my boss. I hated getting up early, going to the office, and being nice to my colleagues. And my relationship wasn't such a great success either. Why did he have to do that? And why didn't he do that? With a rising panic, I noticed that I was growing a little tired of him. But where could I find a good – no, better – replacement in a hurry?

I was not at all satisfied with my life. I had painful periods of worrying about this; they grew ever longer and I sunk ever deeper. I stayed in bed, watched too much tv, fell asleep on the sofa and didn't answer the telephone. I had accepted life as senseless and depressing. All my favorite authors told me I was right. Being happy was watching for just ten seconds a year the sun sinking into the sea, sitting on a tropical beach.

I could have carried on like this forever – or at least until my death. But somewhere in this black pit of misery, something began to vibrate inside me. Something happened around my fortieth birthday. I couldn't take it anymore. I didn't want to be so unhappy anymore and went on a search.

I decided to read other books – no more contemporary literature, but books about philosophy, psychology, spirituality and religion. Many of these books – some more than others – said much the same thing, albeit in different ways.

Being happy is something that we have in our own hands. Being happy has almost nothing to do with things around you and almost everything to do with things inside you. Happiness is not the absence of problems, you can wait forever for that, but being happy despite your problems. It's not about the world, but about your attitude to that world. You can be ungrateful because so many things go wrong. Or grateful for the many good things. You can try to concentrate on the positive things in the world, in others, and in yourself instead of on the negative. You can choose egotism, short-term pleasure and shame, or a wise, sensible, and mature life. Living according to your own standards and values makes you happy.

It almost seems as if you have to be happy in order to become happy. If you are not happy now, you will never be happy. If you cannot see all the good and beautiful things now, you won't see them in the future, no matter how much money, love, success, and fame you achieve. It is all about the way you look at things. What an astonishing thought! So I really don't need to feel miserable anymore? Could there really be an end to that never-ending feeling of unhappiness?

Happiness is something you choose to have – or not. If you don't actively choose, you do what you have always done.

TIPS

- Think what you get out of concentrating on the negative side of everything. Is it familiar? Is it macho? Is it common in your circle?
- How would people react if you concentrated on the positive side of everything? Is that reaction more important than being unhappy?
- The glass is half full and (thus) at the same time half empty. Again, if you don't actively choose, you do what you have always done.

24 DESIRES

"If I had that, I really would be satisfied"

I was feeling bad again. Really bad. As if a heavy black stone was lying in my stomach – the pain was that bad. Everything had failed! I sat thinking and worrying about all the things I didn't have but wanted so badly. If I had those things, I could finally be happy. Jesus, why had I never met the Perfect Partner? Why had the *Times* never begged me to write a column for them (on page 1!)? Why didn't I have the energy, the discipline and the talent to produce a novel every year that would move everybody to amazement? And where, by the way, was my first million?

While I was floundering around in this pitch-black pool, this idea came to me: but wait a minute – everything I wanted five years ago, I've got now! No matter how badly I felt, when I checked that old list of desires, I couldn't do otherwise than conclude that that was the case. Yes, all of it. Not a single exception. I had got it all.

Then why wasn't I happy? No – why was I so unhappy, so desperately unhappy? Well – the reason I was so desperately unhappy was because I had new desires and these had not yet been fulfilled – and I didn't really expect that to happen anytime soon!

Yet whenever I get exactly what I want, I'm still not happy. I'm never satisfied! I once heard a Dutch writer complaining, and I thought at the time: I'd love to have his success and reputation! But is that what he wants? No, he isn't satisfied either and wants the success and reputation of Julian Barnes. And Barnes doesn't just want to be famous in Great Britain, but wants to be V.S. Naipaul. But V.S. Naipaul wants to be the world-famous American author Philip Roth. And Roth would really like to be Tolstoy. And Tolstoy, by the way, wanted to be Jesus Christ. If I suddenly achieved the success and reputation of the Dutch writer, I would be satisfied. But not for long. I would soon want the success of Barnes. And so on.

It seems that satisfying desires is never satisfying. Even though we give up so much for them! We work day and night to get money and status. We forget our family, our friends – we forget everybody if need be. We throw our conscience and our soul into the battle and sell them for some cheap success. And if we get everything that we desire, there is always something new that we want, again at the cost of everything.

And with this last "everything", I mean inner peace. I think that we throw that away, even though that is really what we truly want. That is the only thing that can make us happy. Unfortunately, we think that we can become happy with houses, second homes, cars, jobs, sex, pleasure, children, money, admiration, career, respect, success, reputation, and love from others. But if we satisfy these desires it is not satisfying because these are not true desires. If these were true desires, then we would be satisfied by them.

You never have enough of things you don't really want.

TIPS

- How do you recognise false desires? (1) Desires that you only have in order to belong, to be what they call "successful" in our society. (2) Everything you have to do to satisfy such a desire becomes an irritating burden. (3) After you have "satisfied" that desire, a new one takes its place.
- And how do you recognise true desires? (1) The desire has been with you for a long time, often stemming from the time of your youth. (2) Not only the goal itself, but the way to reaching that goal is satisfying; you wake up in the morning and are eager to do it (enthusiasm, flow). (3) Satisfying such a desire is an ongoing matter, even continuing happily after you have seemingly satisfied it.
- Inner peace has nothing to do with what you have, what status you have, but exclusively with your attitude, the view you take on things (yourself!). Don't satisfy your desires, but change your view.

25 LITTLE VOICE

"You are so stupid!"

I walk around with a little voice in my head from which my worst enemy could learn a lot. That little voice tells me that when somebody pays me a compliment, he doesn't really mean it and if he does mean it, then he isn't really capable of passing an opinion. That little voice tells me that whatever I do at that moment can't be right. Just stop. That little voice tells me that I look terrible, that people are laughing at me, that I am a failure, and that I should be ashamed of myself and feel guilty. That little voice is extremely negative and loves exaggerating and causing pain.

Everything that has gone wrong in my adult life can be laid at the feet of that little voice. I acquiesced in studying law because, "You can't do anything better." I should forget what I really want because, "You won't be able to do it anyway." Others are taken seriously, but the little voice says: "They think you're nothing but a plonker."

Everybody gets negative messages as a child. Whenever I got low marks at school, I had the feeling that I was worthless, a total failure. My friends were always allowed to do everything (or so I thought), but my parents always said no. "Are you sure you know what you're doing?", and the patronizing smile before I had even done anything.

Everybody who sowed doubt with their glances and fed my fear of failure with their remarks has disappeared from my life. But that doesn't matter. I apparently thought this such a pity that I have since taken the place of all these people myself. "Jesus, you look awful!" "Don't bother, you'll never be able to do it!" "Don't you remember that time when everything was such a mess?" "Idiot!"

You act in exactly the way that brings to life the things of which you are afraid. Just before an exam, you walk away because "I'm scared of failing." Yes, if you don't take the exam, you will certainly fail. You don't bother about how you dress, because "I'm so unattractive, it won't make any difference." Yes, anybody who wears such boring clothes automatically becomes unattractive. I don't dare ask because "I'm sure to be turned down." Yes, if you don't ask, then you certainly won't get it, and you have been rejected in advance.

It's crazy that that venomous, destructive, and negative little voice is in my head and judges and sabotages me and makes my life a living hell. I used to think: If you are at peace with everybody, you have inner peace as well. No, inner peace is when you are at peace with yourself, when you don't argue with yourself, when you become your own best friend. In fact, when the little voice disappears.

You don't do that by arguing with the little voice or by wishing it away, but by replacing it with a new voice. By changing the voice of your worst enemy into the voice of your closest friend. If you don't know what that voice would say, you should think of someone who loves you and has your best at heart. What would that person say to you now? Would it be judgmental or encouraging? If you are a believer, it is the voice of Jesus or God.

This is the biggest gift you can give yourself. It doesn't cost a penny, but it does cost an enormous amount of effort.

TIPS

- In what areas do you say things to yourself to keep yourself down, to hold yourself back, things that sabotage your pursuit of your dreams? Write them down.
- Think what a good friend would say to you in these areas. Write that down, too. Say that to yourself every morning and every evening. It would be best to never stop doing it, but persist for at least three weeks.
- What really helps: Look on every other person as a potential friend.

26 NICE

"I say yes, but I really mean no"

At a given moment, I realised that I often say yes when I mean no. "Can you do that for me?" "Can you lend me some money?" "Would you like to drop in on Sunday?" "I've just had a terrible discussion with my boss / partner / father, can we talk?"

I always keep saying yes to these questions when I really mean no. This behaviour is called passive-aggressive: you seem passive, but you're actually aggressive.

Why do I give somebody attention, time, energy, and money if I don't want to? I used to think it was simply because I'm a nice guy. But why then was I irritated when they kept coming back for more? And also irritated if they weren't grateful but instead angry if I was sometimes forced to say no. Was I really that nice?

You do everything for a reason, almost always to get something. If I say yes, I get something, namely that people think of me as nice. I am scared that they won't think of me as nice if I say no, and I hope they will think I'm nice if I give them what they want. Why do I want so desperately for people to think I am nice? Why do I want that more when thinking in retrospect: Damn it, I said yes again when I meant no.

I want people to think I am nice because I am insecure, because I want to be accepted, because I am scared that otherwise I am worth nothing. Apparently I think: If other people think I'm nice, I may also start thinking I am nice.

Unfortunately, it doesn't work. Even if they think I am nice, I still think I am nothing. I am secretly irritated because I feel that they think I am a nice doormat and don't respect me. And I think I'm a proper plonker because I don't dare to say no. I don't do myself any good.

But I realise that I don't do anybody else any good either. I stimulate people to be selfish and irresponsible. They become dependent on me. And those that I help the most become bottomless pits that want and expect more and more from me. They also look on me as successful and find themselves pitiful, something they really hate. What's more, it's better that they discuss the difficulties with their boss / partner / parent / child – with the person concerned and not with me.

They feel from your hidden irritation that you really don't want to give at all. They feel that there are selfish reasons for you saying yes. You want something back in return: their gratitude and for them to think you're a nice person. You have to think I'm nice because I've "paid" for it. That is manipulation. Apparently I'm not nice enough and have to "pay" for friends.

The solution is that I only say yes when I really mean yes. And no when I really mean no. It is better for me, but also better for others.

As soon as you say no, others will respect you even if they may not think you are quite as nice. That's not a problem, because you will start liking yourself more and so others don't have to do it as much as before.

There will hopefully come a time when I can be really nice: giving without wanting anything in return.

TIPS

- Never immediately say yes, but say: "I have to think about it; I'll call you back."
- Set aside one day during which, in principle, you will say no to everybody who wants something from you.
- If you want to say yes and are still in doubt: think what the other can do for you in return and ask them for it.

27 BROODING

"I'm always worrying about things"

Brooding is something that comes easily to me. I wake up at night and then can't get back to sleep. It lasts for hours. Even when I lay awake in bed in the morning, negative thoughts tumble over each other. I hate that person at my work! What on earth should I do about my relationship? If only I had a little more money! It was really dumb to do that! How am I going to solve that? Why am I putting it off for so long? Why did that happen? Why do I stuff myself with food? Why do I spend so much time in front of the box? And why am I so dissatisfied?

What I brood over most is the future. I used to think: Later, when I'm older, later, when I have a job, a house, a partner and children. Then I'll be happy! But I noticed that when I had all that – when I was older, had a job, a house, and a partner – I thought: Later, when I have more success. Later, when I have a villa in the south of France. Later when I'm rich and famous!

My life was one long wait for better times. Once I've achieved that – then... yes, then! But I never enjoyed the better times that had already arrived. My first sexual relationship, my first real job, my first documentary, my first book. Even before the moment arrived when I got all these things, I was worrying about what I didn't yet have. It seemed like I was running a marathon without a finish.

I worry about the future, but also about the past: everything wrong that was done to me, about my youth and teens. At crucial moments in my life I have, with a perfect sense of timing, said or done exactly the wrong thing – or neglected to do the right thing. I've been cowardly, told lies, been my own worst enemy! If I think back to certain things, I feel extremely ashamed and embarrassed.

In short, I brood about the future that isn't yet here and about the past that I cannot change. I have come to the conclusion that brooding is silly, but reflecting on the past and future is useful. I now call reflecting on the past "working through" and reflecting on the future "happily chasing my dreams".

The opposite of living in the past and the future is living in the here and now. I have noticed that that is the best antidote for brooding. When you live in the present moment you notice the little things that life offers us free of charge. The reflection of the sun on water. A loving compliment. A baby in a pram. Falling snowflakes. If you are brooding, you don't notice all that.

I always thought: I will be happy if my wishes come true. No, if my wishes come true, I am still dissatisfied. Let's be happy now. How? The only good question is: What is wonderful in your life right here and now? I have to answer that question every day, no, every single hour. Seize the day.

All that sounds wonderful, but I have to wrestle constantly with it. Brooding comes much easier to me than being happy.

It's a lot more difficult to be happy than unhappy.

TIPS

- Don't try to stop brooding, but force yourself to think of the things that you wanted several years ago and have now got.
- Start making a list of all the things that make your life worthwhile, big things and small things.
- In the morning try to think what you will enjoy most today. At the end of the day, write down three things that you have enjoyed during the day.

28 MASK

"I'm fine, thank you"

There has been a lot of pain and sorrow in my life – at least, that's what I say now. I never used to talk about it. It works like clockwork: If you deny it, it isn't there. I'm fine, thank you. At school I felt lonely and stupid, but I never spoke to anybody about it. At home I lived like a zombie, but if anybody asked me how I was, I answered: "Fine." And later, I told everybody I had had a happy youth and that my relationship was fine. In other words: The Good News Show.

All lies and half truths. Why deny things and tell such lies? Even though nobody had ever told me, I knew perfectly well that I should never show that I was hurt or humiliated, that you had to keep your mouth shut if your work didn't amount to much and your relationship was empty and sad. Nobody must know that I felt forgotten, rejected, and ridiculed, that I actually felt scared of everything and everyone, and that I sometimes felt such a total failure that I had moments of panic. The worse I felt, the louder I denied it.

For a long time, I have put a brave face on things; I was tough, never acknowledged my weaknesses and certainly never asked for help. I thought: If people find me pitiful, I'll be rejected. Or they will show me sympathy and that's a disaster. Then I'm a loser, and I mustn't ever be a loser!

I understand that you are scared of showing your weaknesses, but if we were all honest, we'd know that we are all scared and sad. If we know that it is the same for everybody, it comes as a relief. Everybody has his or her weaknesses; nobody is perfect. Well, in fact everybody has a lot of weaknesses.

This isn't about whether something goes wrong in your life, but what you do about it. The bad side to denial is that if you deny having a painful problem, you can never solve it. Because you don't have a problem. Then you simply repeat the same mistakes and it keeps hurting, time and again. Denial robs you of the solution (and therefore also of achieving your cherished dream) and you are your own worst enemy.

Another disadvantage to denying your weaknesses is that you never really get into contact with others. You only ever show the armour and never the vulnerable flesh it conceals, the real you. All your interactions are then superficial. But if you honestly say something about your weaknesses, two things happen. The plastic yellow bellies flee (bye bye) and you immediately make real contact with the courageous. You aren't ridiculed, but smiled upon. What's more, you no longer have to worry about being unmasked.

Some people, particularly older women, do not wear a mask with a triumphant smile on it, but a victim's mask with a frozen grimace of pain. They host the Bad News Show, which is just as much of a lie.

It is, I think, wise to wear a mask outside. But inside, you can take off the mask. If you discuss important matters with your partner, family, friends, and colleagues and especially with yourself, show your true face. People you love – including yourself – must and should be allowed to see who you really are: the person behind the mask. Without your mask, you are honest, brave, fascinating, and have genuine interactions with others and with yourself. You seem vulnerable, but you are in fact less vulnerable.

Acknowledging weaknesses is the start of the solution and thus not something for losers but for winners.

TIPS

- Is there something you always deny and that obstructs your path? Find somebody dear to you and tell them about it. Say that you are not looking for some profound response, but that you just need to tell them about it.
- You can also do it less officially and, during a pleasant conversation, just casually mention that you were recently reading a book and realised... and so on.
- Have you suddenly had the shocking realisation that you only have superficial chats with people dear to you? Don't question them about intimate matters, but tell them something intimate about yourself. For example, something that you have never dared mention but that you know is true. If it concerns your relationship: Start today!

29 ZOMBIE

"Yes, sure, okay, fine"

When I think about my youth, I see a quiet, withdrawn boy – somebody that people smilingly call a "dreamer" – watching from the sidelines and never participating. Before then, there were certainly moments when I screamed and kicked, but from the moment I became aware of myself there is a black hole. Who is that boy? What did he like doing? What did he dream about? I don't recognise that person I see in my past. I don't know who he is.

When I was a child, I automatically tagged along. I had one friend, and the only reason we connected was that neither of us really belonged; we didn't really like each other but were condemned to each other, and we both knew it. Not a single subject at school really interested me and I had no hobbies or passions such as sports or collecting things. If, during that time, you had asked me what I really wanted, I would have answered: "Don't know." But nobody ever posed that question. And so I didn't pose it myself either. Children see and treat themselves in the same way their parents see and treat them.

In retrospect, it seems as if I was in a depression between the ages of ten and thirty. If apathy, boredom, and joylessness are characteristics of depression, then I was depressed. I did what I was told, never became excited about anything, but never put up a fight either. I was half alive, uninspired, emotionless, listless, a zombie. Later I called that, revealingly, shy and introvert.

As a teenager, I often felt empty and helpless, and the periods I felt like that lasted longer and longer. Then, as a student, I slept too much, even in the afternoon, and I sat endlessly in front of the television stuffing my face. I was lonely and cynical, never enthusiastic, proud, or happy.

I was half alive, and therefore half dead. And in this way, I got through my studies and had various jobs and relationships, including the relationship with myself. I led my whole life like that! Apathetic, indifferent, unmotivated, half asleep, satisfied with little or even less, and accepting this vague, dull pain as something that had always been there and was my lot. You become enthusiastic if you know what you would like to do and what your dreams are. But I never heard or posed these questions. Who was I? Silence. What did I feel? Huh? What did I really want? Don't know. I was nothing and wanted nothing.

Until a crisis came and I had to ask myself what I really wanted. I didn't get an answer. I had to learn to be honest with myself, just as you have to learn to swim. Weeks, months later, answers started dribbling through and I slowly came to know myself – after my fortieth birthday. I learned to know my dreams and become enthusiastic. About my work, my relationship, about myself and about the life I wanted to lead. I even took risks to achieve my most cherished dream and suddenly my life became exciting.

I had woken up from my half sleep and started to live.

TIPS

- What things did you like in your youth? Drawing? Cooking? Carpentry? Music? Can you translate that into something you could do now?
- What things come easily to you, so easily, in fact, that you are amazed that others can't do them? What activities make you get out of bed in the morning with an excited feeling? Could you turn this – or something that is similar to this – into a hobby or your work?
- Write down what you would like three friends to say at your funeral. The first begins: "When he finally discovered what he really wanted, he..." The second says: "To our amazement, he stopped doing everything and then turned to..." And the third begins: "We all knew that he secretly wanted to... and what a pity that he never got round to it."

30 IN LOVE

"Oh, I'm so happy!"

When, several years ago, I fell in love I thought: it's quite a coincidence that I should fall in love just when my relationship has turned sour and I'm ready for it. Now I realise that the reverse was true: I fell in love because my relationship had turned so sour. Unconsciously, I was looking for a substitute for my existing partner.

Falling in love is just like falling asleep: you can't force it but you can create all the necessary conditions to allow it to happen. For falling asleep that means being tired, a nice warm bed, and not lying there brooding. For falling in love that means going out, flirting, and opening yourself up to it. Unconsciously, I gave myself permission – perhaps even the assignment – to find a new partner.

When the spark ignited, I found myself, as usual, in a strange mood. Being in love turns my body and mind crazy. I live on a cloud, I look at everything through rose-coloured glasses, the other person is perfect, I am no longer myself – and it is in exactly that frame of mind that I take the major decision to enter into a relationship. If you are already in a relationship, then that relationship will end. If you have children, then they're going to be on the receiving end.

Scientific research has shown that certain chemical substances in your body are involved in falling in love, but these cease to be active after three to six months. But by then you've moved in together, everybody expects you to be happy, perhaps somebody is pregnant, and you may have bought a house together. Looking through your rose-coloured spectacles, you attach to the other person all the qualities that you want to see, because you need them, but which the other person doesn't have, or may only have in limited amounts. You are like a selfish child who demands that the other make you happy. Some people fall in love with somebody they only know over the internet. If the other person doesn't join in the game, they become angry and sad.

Once the infatuation has passed, you see the other person for what they are and you are disappointed. He always arrives late, she always watches stupid tv programmes, he farts, she isn't perfect. It was all an illusion.

While love is conscious and rational, being "in love" is unconscious and irrational. It is a disease with symptoms that are more or less identical for everybody. Eating, sleeping, and thinking are disturbed, just like in every crisis. Falling in love seems like a trick of nature to get us to procreate and being in love has, therefore, a lot to do with sex. I only fall in love with people I find sexually attractive.

And I always fall in love with somebody who, in one way or another, resembles my parents in appearance, character or some other way and is thus *familiar*. That's why people always say: During our first conversation it was as if I had known him or her all my life!

Some people say that in this way you can relive and ultimately solve any unresolved problems that you may have with your parents (and we all have those). But if, for example, your parents were emotionally disturbed and the partner that you have now chosen is also like that, because that is so familiar, then you've got a problem. If that happens, the old wound gets a hard kick and that's why it's so painful.

Being in love is selfish, horny, childish, addictive, romantic, dependent, dishonest, manic, diseased, unconscious, irrational, temporary, drunk, and blind.

"In love" is the very opposite to "love".

TIPS

- If you are in love: Listen carefully to what the people who know you say, and take your loved one everywhere with you.
- Don't make any decisions that cannot easily be reversed in six months' time.
- Realise that, in one way or another, you are drunk and that your vision is seriously distorted.

If you think all of this is nonsense, then you'll know for sure you're in love.

31 COMPETITION

"Holy crap, she's having more success than me!"

Sometimes I think that everything that has gone wrong in my life – and is still going wrong in it – is due to the fact that I consider my life a competition. My private life, but especially my professional life, is an ongoing competition, and one, I am afraid, that I am losing.

I'd like to be handsome, but that won't happen. Every time I see a picture of myself, I am convinced of the fact. I'm not handsome, not at all; I am ugly! I dream of being so remarkably handsome that everybody immediately falls under my spell at the very first meeting.

I have always wanted to become a famous author who is admired by all, is invited everywhere, and is treated with respect. Somebody like Salman Rushdie. I'm not a fan of his, but perhaps I should think about my motives: Don't I like him because I'm jealous? Or maybe I would prefer to be Houellebecq. I'm no fan of his either, but why do I think it so necessary to mention that?

Because I didn't think I was good enough as a writer, I ended up in television. And there I worked on well-known shows and with prestigious hosts, but I don't feel as if their quality or popularity had anything to do with me. Otherwise they would have done their best to keep me close at hand, and they didn't bother. They kept other people. That I suspect those other people of sucking up and mindlessly going along is something else that I should take a hard look at.

And so I have lost every competition in my life. I'm no longer young but old; I have a law degree but I'm no great lawyer; I'm sometimes amusing, but no Rowan Atkinson. I have the occasional original idea but I'm no Pauline Kael. I'm not poor, but unfortunately, I don't have the money of Bill Gates. I write adequately, but I am no C.S. Lewis.

The annoying thing is that if you consider life, your life, a competition, you basically always lose. There is always somebody else who does things better, who is better than you. There is always somebody who is better-looking, younger, has a more attractive partner, richer, more famous, more powerful, in other words, more successful. Comparison is lethal.

Just imagine that you actually win and are the best, then everybody else who took part are automatically losers. They become your enemies. If you do that with your partner, you may have won the competition but you will have lost a partner and together you will have lost your relationship.

If there is one interesting competition it is not with others but with yourself. The competition to allow your potential to flourish, to discover your real talents, to become yourself as far as it is possible. Then you don't need to be better than others, simply the best you can be, faithful only to yourself. I don't, by the way, call that a competition, but rather allowing the possibility for growth.

What's more, the fact is that if you regard life as a competition you perform less well than if you regard it as a possibility for growth. In a competition you are nervous, scared that others are better and that you could lose; after all, there can only be one winner. If you don't need to win but just grow, you won't be nervous or afraid and will thus perform better.

See life not as a competition but as a possibility for growth and you will always win.

TIPS

- Stop comparing yourself to others.
- Wish other people success, in your head and out loud.
- Live according to your own desires – do the work that you enjoy, choose a partner you like, and live your own life.

32 INTELLECTUAL

"I am more intellectual than you"

When I was a student, I also came to see being intellectual and cultural as a competition. You could go see *The Sound of Music*, but Fellini's *Satyricon* was, of course, much more artistic. You could read Stephen Fry, but Bernard Levin was far more intellectual. You could read the *Sun*, but the *Times* was far more prestigious. Nobody had ever explained that to me, but I was acutely aware of where the dividing line was drawn. If you thought one was good, you were respectable. If you found the other good, you were looked down upon.

But I soon realised that this was not true and I considered it important to tell everybody, "completely honestly" that I, yes me who was so intelligent and had such exquisite taste, actually enjoyed *Game of Thrones*. And that I enjoyed run-of-the-mill pop music, adored

Hollywood action movies, and that my favourite food was fast food. I was a so-called lover of nonsense and proudly looked down on all those culture snobs that preferred atonal music, Kieslowski, and BBC Three.

Because of my background and environment, I was automatically one of the elite, but, or perhaps because of that, I saw through them. They congratulated themselves and each other on their profound predilections and intellectual taste. But I laughed at them. No Disney for them, but obscure and incomprehensible Czech black and white arthouse films. No page-turners, but Goethe and Schopenhauer. No Abba, but Frank Zappa. They were hypocritical social climbers who did not rise because of money, power, or fame, but through cultural capital.

While I amused myself with their lies, I could forget my own. Of course, I could enjoy Seneca and Montaigne. My brain was quickly tired of *People Magazine* and my stomach of fast food. I wanted stronger stuff. When I worked in television and could choose between a quiz and a talk show, I chose the latter. And when I could choose between a talk show and a documentary, I again chose the latter.

But what's behind all this? I am an intellectual and at the same time I am not. I like to listen to Coldplay, but also to Bach. I like Anthony Trollope but also Garfield. I like Ingmar Bergman, but also *Close Encounters*. You're an ordinary human being that eats, makes love, prays, cries, sleeps, drives a car, and enjoys the normal things. At the same time, you're somebody that listens to certain music and reads certain books. I think that I am 90 percent an ordinary person and 10 percent an intellectual. Often superficial, without nuance, and childish; sometimes profound, subtle, and adult.

What we witness in the so-called elite are people who desperately try to be intellectual not for ten percent of the time, but for the full one hundred percent. They go exclusively to the right films, read exclusively the right newspaper, have exclusively intellectual friends

95

with whom they exclusively discuss the right books in the exclusively right manner. They deprive themselves of many things.

A true intellectual realises that he is only intellectual some of the time.

TIPS

- Some people will no matter what it takes become rich or famous or powerful. Others want in this way to belong to the intellectual and cultural elite. How do you feel watching the right film, reading the right book and visiting your intellectual friends?
- It is the same as for people who want to be rich: You must realise that once you have overcome the obstacles (if you can) and become part of the elite, you will never again be satisfied and will always worry about the next obstacle. So do you really want to?
- Try to discover what you really really enjoy and realise that it is not a question of either / or but of and / and.

33 DISSATISFIED

"I always want something else"

When I have work to do, I want to be done with it as quickly as possible. That stupid job that you have to go to every day and where you have to do things that you don't enjoy doing. And all those annoying colleagues and that authoritarian boss that without exception I grow to despise. If only I could stop! So, I stop. But after three days at home, I start missing the regularity and liveliness of my work and I become downhearted that I am no longer busy doing things and earning money.

I experience something similar in relationships. When I'm with somebody, I dream of being alone, feeling free, and doing exactly what I feel like doing instead of wearing this tight collar that restricts your every movement. What on earth have I got myself into? But when, after much pain and sorrow, I am alone again, in a week or so I'm yearning for that one true love to make me happy, fall deliriously in love and do lots of nice things together.

That's the way it happens with everything. The person I'm dining with in a restaurant has always chosen something that looks more appetising than what I have on my plate. I've only just started a holiday – it happens at the airport – and I want to get back to my own familiar house and things. But on the way back, and once I've reached home, I long to return to the sun, the exotic food, and the liberating absence of everyday concerns.

I often think: I'm really unlucky, never in the right place and always wanting something else. Everybody is satisfied with their lives except me. I always choose the wrong thing!

Until I realised that it has nothing to do with my work, nothing to do with my partner, nothing to do with my holiday, and nothing, either, to do with the dish I chose. It's something in me. I am always nagging and complaining because I concentrate on what I don't have and what I'm not. If I give that all my attention, I only see what is not good and don't see what is good. And finally, I convince myself that nothing at all is right. And then it's always better in the past, in the future, somewhere else, and particularly when it comes to the neighbours. The grass is always greener on the other side.

This way of looking at things may seem innocent, but it slowly and surely eats at my life. It's much better and more honest to look at what I do have and who I really am, and to consider how good and valuable that actually is. I have noticed that if I look sensibly at things – an extremely difficult task for me – then I see that my grass is really quite green and the grass in the past, in the future, somewhere else and particularly that on the other side is withered and scorched.

And if my grass really isn't green enough, I should stop looking on the other side and start watering my lawn.

TIPS

- Name three things that are good in your life.
- What do you do better now than in the past?
- What enjoyable thing are you going to do today?

34 PLEASURE

"Fun? Can't get enough!"

I was born in 1954 and was thus one of the first Dutch people who grew up in a time of abundance. For the first time, we lived like kings and queens. There was more than enough food, modern education, and medical care for everybody, less and less religion and more and more free time, and oppressed groups such as women and gays were given a voice. I considered this perfectly normal and was thus naïve and spoiled.

When at the age of nineteen I became a student and left home, I chose to live in Amsterdam, because I knew there was lots of fun to be found there. I was mad about sex, films, music, reading, and having fun. Studying for ten years was an acceptable excuse to be able to do all these things without reservation. At that time, Holland was changing from a childish, innocent and poor fifties society into an individualistic, juvenile and rich seventies society. In addition to unmasking the pedantic hypocrisy of those in power, adolescents have another characteristic: in reaction to their so-called dull and boring parents, they fortunately discover fun. But alas, they then upgrade it to the main aim in life.

I joined in enthusiastically. If it was suddenly allowed, it had to be immediately experienced. The world changed. We had to enjoy life more by working less, listening to much more pop music, using drugs, partying, and practising free sex. Uninhibited enjoyment!

But after all that enjoyment, I was increasingly left with a vague, alien feeling. Is this all there is? What now? I always thought that that feeling meant: Come on, find another, more intense enjoyment. More daring sex, more partying, or stronger drugs.

I noticed that the more I chased after fun, the higher dose of it I needed. It was never enough. Initially, I was only bored and morose when the hangover set in, but then I became bored when I was supposed to be enjoying myself. Going out became an expensive, compulsive obligation, sex became a boring routine, and listening to music something automatic that went by almost unnoticed. I realised that I was not making love with my body, but with my head that was saying: "More sex!" And I didn't eat and drink with my body – that is, with my mouth and overfull stomach – but with my head that said: "Eat more, drink more." I continued despite a lonely, empty feeling of discontent. Is that addiction?

It cost a lot of empty and depressing "fun" to finally realise that it would not make me happy. Cicero wrote: "It is not through levity, lust, play, and laughter, those companions of lightheartedness, that somebody becomes happy, but through fortitude and perseverance, even when he is sorrowful." Resisting strongly, I gradually became convinced that I would not become happy by chasing unbridled pleasure for years on end, but by becoming virtuous, by acting sensibly, responsibly, wisely, and maturely.

As I write this, I see more and more spoiled children, entitlement and people indulging themselves. These things are becoming more common while boredom and dissatisfaction grow. Pleasure is seriously overestimated.

It is, by the way, very sensible and mature to chase after pleasure. As long as it really does give you pleasure.

TIPS

- Try not doing something pleasurable for a couple of days, and then go back to it again. Isn't moderation in all things the spice of life?
- Buy a new board game; there are some really good ones around. Play with the whole family. Invite people round for a game. There are all sorts of game clubs.
- Instead of chasing after pleasure, give up your time to do something for somebody else. How does that feel afterwards?

35 KIND

"Being kind is rather scary"

I'm scared of compliments, intimacy, warmth, admiration and people who touch me. I'm scared of all expressions of affection from others who are – or want to be – kind to me. Particularly if they are genuine. How on earth should I react to them? I stutter, I blush, I fidget, I feel small, I shift around, and make light of it or do not believe it ("don't be silly, you're exaggerating"). I even get it with good friends. If somebody's kind to me, I cringe, it almost hurts.

So not only negative emotions cause me problems, but positive ones as well. My absent father – the parent that was the most emotional – expressed his affection by pinching me and my brothers hard. Being kind was odd, nasty, unfamiliar. If a film star started moaning "I love you," I immediately felt ashamed for them. Nothing was ever said about it, but as a child I understood that expressing kind emotions and the behaviour associated with it was exaggerated, hysterical, and affected. Thank goodness that we were so composed and correct at home.

When I was a film critic, I once, after spending months on end trashing every film, wrote a positive review. The editor immediately asked me: "Hey, do you mean we should really go see that film?" The implication was clear: We are critical and hip and only say what's wrong with a film. The same was true for me as an employee: I only heard anything when I had done something wrong. I accepted that as the most normal thing in the world.

We live in a world where people shout at each other about their driving, complain about earning too little, whine about how unjust the world is, insult others that are wrong and grumble that it's all crap. I'm like that with everybody, but especially with myself: "You see – you're awful! Stupid prick!"

I once had a session with a psychiatrist who said: "François, say out loud: I am a nice guy." Silence. I looked at him, gulped for breath, wanted to say it, but I couldn't do it! If he had asked me to say "I'm a terrible guy" I could have said it straight away. I'm exceptionally good at being critical with myself, I do it the whole day, my whole life, and was shown how to do it at home. But being kind to others or myself is like speaking a foreign language.

I say that I like gentle people and a kind partner, but I look down on them. I look up at dominant people who are critical of me. That is familiar, no matter how painful the criticism may be.

Dear reader, the world is upside down! Criticism is familiar and being kind is painful. I can carry on being terribly tough, but let me be kind for a change, no matter how unfamiliar, unbelievable, and scary it might be. Because secretly, I would love for somebody to stroke my hair. Particularly myself.

TIPS

- If you want to be kind to somebody else, force yourself to do it, if only once, no matter how difficult it may be and no matter how awkwardly / indifferently / dismissively the other may react.
- If you want to be kind to yourself, force yourself to do it, if only once, no matter how difficult it may be and no matter how awkwardly / indifferently/dismissively you may react.
- If somebody is kind to you, try just once to react with style. The least you can do is say thank you. The best is to make a party of it. And if your partner / best friend / intimate family member isn't kind to you: Ask them whether they can please be kind to you in the future.

36 PROCRASTINATION

"I'll do it later"

There is a little boy inside me who starts screaming and stamping his foot if he doesn't get his way. He feels a little peckish, calls it hunger, and demands that something is immediately fetched or bought, or taken away from somebody else. That doesn't only apply to (fast!) food, but also to drugs, drink, texting and driving at the same time, watching tv and YouTube, lazing around, sleeping in / not going to work, being right, quick sex, buying something, gossiping, becoming angry – anything that gives short-term satisfaction.

That impatient little boy is the boss and has caused a lot of damage. He has raised immediate gratification (such as watching tv) and postponing difficult but necessary duties (such as working) to an art. If he notices that I don't want to postpone an "exhausting" job for once, he starts whining: "I don't feel like it. Please! Do it later! I want to do something nice and easy!"

My whole life is made up of postponing all sorts of difficult things. Not doing your homework now, but listening to music. Not studying but doing something else – vacuuming if necessary. Not sorting out all those papers but clipping my toenails. Not exercising, not that nasty but necessary telephone call, and particularly not thinking about that nagging, threatening problem.

The damage is not so much that short-term satisfaction is so transitory, but that you can never do short and long-term things simultaneously. So, if you arrange your life on a short-term basis, you don't do things for the long-term. You then postpone matters that require effort now, such as following a training course, counting to ten, making an investment, raising a child, or building up a relationship. Postponing means missing out on long-term satisfaction, missing out on reaping the rewards later.

The satisfaction from watching tv comes a lot quicker than from reading, but I always close a book with a feeling of contentment, while an evening watching tv is like eating a big bag of sweets – it makes you nauseous, isn't nutritious, and leaves you with an empty feeling. Eating fast food is nice but unhealthy, and perhaps it's not really so tasty after all. If you really want to eat well, you have to take the time to buy good ingredients and then prepare them carefully into something you enjoy. The first promises satisfaction, the second actually delivers it. Quick sex is nice, but once you have tasted the joys of long, relaxed love-making, quick sex seems like a gymnastic exercise.

So, you can choose between the advantages of short-term enjoyment and long-term enjoyment. Short-term enjoyment means enjoyment now and not later. And long-term enjoyment means enjoying later and not now.

Or so you would think. If you think you're having short-term enjoyment, you aren't really enjoying yourself, because during the so-called enjoyment you are wrestling with a bad conscience. I'll have to work twice as hard later; I'll still be out of shape later; I really should be working right now; how will I handle that increasingly awkward discussion later? And so it's not an option because short-term enjoyment isn't enjoyment at all, in contrast to long-term enjoyment. You can spend your whole life postponing things, even finally starting a demanding but authentic, mature and exciting life.

Don't wait for the "right moment"; that never comes, because the right moment is always now.

TIPS

- Decide what comes top of your list of things you always postpone.
- Think how you could actually do it and don't start on it without preparation. For example: First have something to eat and drink, a quick visit to the loo, turn off the phones, in other words, get rid of all the excuses.
- Do what you've been postponing for an hour and don't accept any interruption! After an hour you're done and you can stop. Set the alarm.

37 MONEY

"I'd be happy with a million"

Money is a problem for most people: There is never enough. They are perfectly convinced that they would be happy with a million. But as soon as they have some money, they spend more than they have. Life is so expensive! But no matter how much they earn and spend, they remain dissatisfied. The real problem they have with money is that they think that spending money gives them satisfaction.

I suffer from the opposite disease. At home, I was a very careful little boy. My brother, who got money from everywhere, never had a penny, but I always had something left over from my pocket money. When I was studying, I was amazed that not everybody was as careful with the little money they had. "What? You've run out of money? How?" The other person apparently didn't know either. When I went to work, I was amazed that nothing changed. Many of my colleagues had, as usual, run out.

I increasingly began to look down on these impulsive and chaotic people who couldn't handle their money, who were only happy when they had spent it all. Slowly I began to understand that wealth had little to do with income and much to do with policy. If you want to be rich, then there's a simple plan: Of course, earn as much as possible, but in particular spend as little as possible.

That's what I did, but I noticed that the more money I had, the less I spent and the more I wanted. I became a miser, in terms of my own spending and on behalf of others. What I noticed was that I never had enough. Once you've got ten thousand in the bank, you want twenty thousand. And if you've got a hundred thousand, you want two hundred thousand. And if you've got two hundred thousand, you want a million. It gives a perverse feeling of power, perhaps similar to people with anorexia nervosa. You deny yourself everything and that hurts, but at the some time it gives a feeling of order and control, a feeling of power.

I was addicted to saving; it became compulsive. Even though I knew at a certain moment that I was working against myself, spending money was something that caused an almost physical pain. I told myself that I needed all that money just in case something happened. But if something happened, I still didn't spend a penny. It's similar to people who are addicted to spending money and feel pain when they can't buy what they "really want".

Only later did I realise that excessive spending was just as stupid as excessive saving. I'm just as greedy as the people who are always penniless. They are greedy for things, because they always want to buy something new, and I am greedy for money, because I always want to have more.

And they both have the same cause: trying to fill an emptiness. Both addictions – excessive spending and excessive saving – give an illusion of happiness. It is an illusion because it is doesn't give any satisfaction. Otherwise we would, at a certain moment, be satisfied and stop constantly wanting more money or more things. But you never have enough money, whether you horde it or spend it. More is never enough.

The only satisfying way to fill the emptiness is to find peace with who you are and what you have.

TIPS

- For people who spend money like there's no tomorrow: make a list of everything you own. Will the next purchase make you happy? Decide to save a set amount automatically each month (through a standing order with your bank, so that you don't have to do anything about it).
- For the misers: make a list of your money and how much your things are worth. Will more savings make you happy? Decide to spend money each month on something nice, for example, a good sweater, a holiday, a massage, an expensive art book, a present for someone, a donation to a charity.
- Look around you, at nature, at your body, at all the things you have in your house, that water flows from the tap, your children, the food on the table – think of something, and be grateful.

38 RELATIONSHIP

"You've got to have a relationship"

Having a relationship is just like having a job and having a house and having children – it's something you have to have. Without all these things, something's not quite right; you have to give an explanation. At least, that's what I thought. Just like almost all important matters in life, I started on this like a bull in a china shop. If you are unprepared when you start on such important matters, you are your own worst enemy. With relationships, I have made every mistake possible. Everybody keeps repeating the same mistakes, but fortunately there are some who write them down. There were books like that around when I made my mistakes, but I never read them. I considered myself far too smart for that.

The first relationship mistake I made was that I felt lonely and wanted a partner who liked me and would treat me well. Who listened to me and said encouraging things to me. A partner who respected me and held me in high regard. In short, somebody who loved me. All the things I wanted from a partner I never gave to myself. And exactly because I never gave them to myself I wanted them badly from somebody else. I never got enough attention and affection from my partner.

I never got enough because I never believed all those nice things they said about me, or at least, not longer than a minute. That's why I wanted more and more. And that's why I drove that partner crazy, causing them to break off the relationship. They could give, but all the love just fell through the bottom, because there simply wasn't any bottom in me. That bottom is called self-trust, self-respect, self-love. "I think you're kind and beautiful" is only something you believe if you think yourself kind and beautiful.

What I have just described is what people mean with: You must first have a relationship with yourself before you can have a relationship with somebody else. I always thought that sounded a little airy-fairy, and indeed it does. But it is just as true as the law of gravity. That law is always valid for everybody everywhere, so also for you. How should you have a relationship with yourself? Read the chapter "Self-love".

My second relationship mistake was that I thought I was looking for a partner who was stronger than me. Even though it seemed that way at the start, it soon became clear that I was the stronger party. Although I was sad about it, it happened in every new relationship. I had a big mouth and I soon had a relationship in which I was the parent and the other was the child. As soon as I had used my dominant, egotistical, and arrogant behaviour to make the other dependent and childish, I became annoyed that the other was so dependent and childish. Dominant people create dependent people. And my partners, in turn, became annoyed that they had become so dependent and became secretly or openly rebellious. Nobody likes it when your partner bosses you around. And so the relationships once again came to an end.

In our emancipated society, I see men who are increasingly less dominant and, as a result, women jump in to fill the gap, play the boss, and thereafter and therefore despise their husband.

A final word: You may have heard that you have to work on your relationship. If there are problems, such as the ones described above, solve them. Solving problems means working because it costs effort. Like respecting each other, being equal, talking about difficult and painful matters, giving something up and being honest.

Most people who have a relationship ... don't have a relationship.

TIPS

- A relationship with yourself is saying nice things to yourself, but more importantly doing nice things for yourself. Stand up for yourself, say what you really want, give yourself something you would like to get from another.
- What has your partner been asking for year after year that you haven't done? Do it now. And give to your partner without wanting something in return.
- Dr Phil says: "Think to yourself every morning: How can I improve my relationship today?"

39 ENVY

"Envious? Me?"

Envy is an emotion that never used to bother me. Or so I thought. Officially, I had nothing against foreigners, but there was quite a racist dissatisfaction lurking in me. They only come here for social benefits, they are getting ruder and ruder, the government is sucking up to them, and just look at how those women dress!

I smiled at my colleagues, but inside I had to force down the rage. Jesus, he's got the job even though he's a lot younger than me! I noticed that, even with my friends, I was bitchy and irritable. That good job, those junkets, the inheritance, the big house, the close relationship, the happy children. Why did they have all that?

Sometimes my thoughts about envy were confused. The Islamic women who are brought here are, of course, scared to death and probably mean well. Those colleagues have had to wait just as long as me and why should I begrudge them the chance? And that big house belonging to my friends is also a burden on their shoulders. Ah, we're all exactly the same: We all want a bit of happiness. But why was I so racist, so angry, so bitchy? Did it have anything to do with them? Did it have something to do with me? I'm afraid that it had everything to do with me.

Behind all those negative emotions lurks my eternal and pervasive fear that I am being deprived of something. Behind my racism is the fear that foreigners may do better than me, that they get more success, respect, and money than me. Behind my fury at work lurks the fear that my colleagues may get their hands on the job that I could do with and by doing that leave no place, money, or applause for me. Behind my irritation at my friends lurks my fear that I will never match their conventional satisfaction and happiness. I am envious!

I am scared that I won't get what I want, what I so desperately want, scared that I'm not good enough to get it, that, just like in the past, I'll be ridiculed and passed over. I'm scared that others will get there before me and that I won't be able to join in, that I will powerlessly have to look on at how others time and time again get what they want and that once again, I won't. I'm scared that I'll lose the competition, be a loser, and remain unhappy for ever.

If I carry on concentrating on what I don't have and what others do have, I'll carry on being jealous and bring down my own house around me. By being afraid that I won't get it and thus expecting that, I actually make sure it happens. By begrudging others their share, I act negatively and they will react negatively towards me and thus will give me nothing.

If I think I'm being deprived of something, I shouldn't think: They shouldn't have it either! No, I should think: They are really welcome to it, *and so am I.*

The less envious I am and the more I want others to have something, the more I receive myself.

TIPS

- Be grateful for what you have. Reflect on how many things you really don't want if you think honestly about it.
- Devise a detailed plan on paper for all those things you really want and immediately put it into practice.
- Ask others who have something you want to help you get it as well.

40 CRYING

"Crying is for wimps"

Several years ago, I was busy in the kitchen. I felt gloomy (that's what I called it then) and something powerful was trying to force its way out. All at once, the constraints that were constricting my throat couldn't keep their grip and everything erupted. It was as if a large concrete dam had suddenly turned out to be paper; the water tore its way through in bucketfuls.

In the week that followed, I cried several times a day and anything was enough to start me off: a lame dog, a sentimental film, an episode of *Children's Hospital*. I had the feeling that I was crying to make up for lost time, as if all those tears that I had blinked back through the years had been kept in a large bottle and the immovable cork had finally popped.

Emotions were alien in my childhood home, little green Martians that didn't exist. Expressing anger was taboo ("hysterical"), just as expressing sorrow ("girlish") and fear ("childish"). Mental pain was something that simply didn't exist. But a spot of blood or physical pain and there were cries of despair and with great sympathy and attention, a plaster was applied. If you were sad, nothing happened. Nobody spoke about feelings and nobody expressed them. If we saw somebody crying on tv, we were all embarrassed and secretly hoped that it would be over quickly. Not a word was spoken about it, except to ridicule it.

I knew nobody who handled emotions in a healthy way. My friends were just like me. Films and tv were sentimental and infantile. Dutch theatre handled emotions as if they were made of plywood. Even books – the only thing at the time that could have saved me – did not shed any light.

The consequences were that I often felt as if I had a brick in my stomach, but always kept the tears in check. That is, until I failed my A levels. I felt lonely and stupid and hated to have to spend another year at this school. I cycled home from school and, for the first time in years, began to sob my heart out. When I reached home, things had returned to normal.

Between the ages of twenty and forty I don't think I cried once. You didn't do it. Crying was childish, emotional, pitiful, theatrical, showing your weaknesses, admitting that something had gone wrong, and acknowledging that you were a loser. No, I'm strong, manly, and everything is just wonderful!

And so I went through life isolated from my own emotions. A feeling only had to raise its head and it was immediately decapitated. By never expressing my emotions, I neglected them to such a degree that they no longer seemed to exist.

I think that your feelings are there to clarify something about yourself and your situation. You mustn't deny emotions, but you must also not allow yourself to be ruled by them. If you allow yourself to be guided by your emotions, there is a great chance that you will act impulsively, childishly, selfishly, or hysterically. Let your head make the final decision, but listen carefully to your heart. If you deny your feelings and don't do anything with them, you become rigid and inflexible. You act as if you feel nothing, so you are not yourself, you are artificial, you wear a mask. I was an emotional invalid, lacked part of myself, and walked around like a robot.

Until that moment in the kitchen. I could no longer avoid it and, with my hand reaching out to the work surface for support, I felt my sorrow and cried.

It was an enormous relief. I didn't have to suppress it any longer. I took off my mask and decided that I wouldn't be embarrassed anymore. Since then I cry regularly and no longer feel silly but in touch with my emotions and afterwards relieved.

TIPS

- Are you embarrassed when somebody cries? Are you scared of crying yourself? Don't wait for the explosion, but let it come. Help yourself by watching tearjerkers.
- When you feel sad, accept it completely. When you cry accept it completely.
- You can also help yourself by surrounding yourself with beauty, such as beautiful music, beautiful nature, happy ends, beautiful sex – and then cry tears of joy.

41 GOD

"What? Ridiculous!"

My parents belonged to the generation that with considerable fuss had wrestled themselves free from the faith of their forefathers. Religion was the opium of the people. The church was just as bad as capital, and both had to be fought fiercely. "The world had to become better!"

Despite the fact that my mother had wrestled herself free of Catholicism and my father had done the same with Protestantism, they still sent me to Sunday school on several occasions. There, I enjoyed listening to the stories from long ago and far away which the Sunday school teacher told with such enthusiasm. She was, by the way, my first and only teacher who was enthusiastic. Her enthusiasm was contagious, just as a lack of enthusiasm would prove with all those other teachers. She told things as if she had experienced them herself and always said, "It all really happened."

Since then, God has always been something of which I have fond childhood memories and at the same time, imitating my parents, I ridiculed. But I preferred to forget the former; people who did something with God in churches, on tv, or on your doorstep were silly idiots who – how on earth could they? – believed in "all that nonsense". If God really exists, why does he allow all those terrible things to happen and, in all his "omnipotence", does nothing about it? After all, wasn't the world supposed to get better?

At Sunday school, I had got to know God as a kind old man with a beard, a bit like Father Christmas, who had created us and sat up there in heaven on his golden throne. If I wanted to talk to him, I had to go to church and pray. On a number of occasions, I went with the girl next door to a Catholic church and found it wonderful – the surroundings, the atmosphere, the common people. God would surely make the world better for these nice, anxious children.

When, for a few months, I worked for the Dutch Evangelical Broadcasting Company, I noticed that they too believed in this Father Christmas God. It is a childishly concrete faith that takes the stories in the Bible literally, that believes that Jesus "really existed", and that God is a sort of person, somebody who is sometimes kind (a surrogate mother) and sometimes strict (a surrogate father).

No, I don't believe in that God, an old, holy man that created the world and looks down on us. God is not a person but an idea, not concrete but abstract. God didn't create us, we created God. God is the idea that there is much good in the world, that mankind is capable of a lot of good. God is our belief in that, our conscience, our hope, our comfort, our best selves, our wisdom, the best in us, all the good deeds that we do.

God is knowing that we have to do our best to make something of it, that we must fight for justice. God is a virtuous life of reasonable and mature men and women. God is not something outside ourselves, but something inside ourselves. God is love and truth. What God wants (the good) is more important than what we want (our own interests). God is our heart and our soul. God is knowing that pleasure and art and sex and conviviality and friendship and love and music and children are wonderful. God is knowing that nature, the world and the universe are often breathtakingly beautiful. God is knowing that our body, our mind, and this life are miracles. God is laughing through the tears. God – that is us – must make the world better! I sincerely believe in that.

I believe in God.

TIPS

- Try not to let your ideas and feelings about God and religion be dictated by what your parents told you, whether good or bad.
- What people blame on religion is often justified, but perhaps we should blame the church and the people who created and create it.
- Try to make the world better, with or without God.

42 FORGIVENESS

"I'll get you!"

I once saw a young woman on tv talking about how she was systematically hurt and abused by what seemed to be an extremely frightening man. She had suppressed her pain for a long time, but it didn't leave her in peace and when she finally acknowledge the extent of the problem, she first became incredibly angry and then was sad for a long time afterwards. Anyway, one day she went to the house of the man concerned and rang his doorbell. The last shots were filmed from some distance. He opened the door and she calmly told him that she had forgiven him.

I was flabbergasted by the end of the story. The filthy rat in the doorway had got off lightly! But later I realized that a crueller punishment doesn't exist. Those words she uttered caused more pain than if she had screamed and shouted at the man. If that had happened he could have thought: What a loudmouth! and would have been able to concentrate fully on that. Now the man could hardly be annoyed at the woman and had to concentrate on what she was saying and thus on what he had done to her. What's more, if somebody forgives you in such a reasonable, sensible, and wise manner, then there must be at least a germ of truth in the words.

This is one of life's many paradoxes. The girl didn't want to punish the man, but that meant she did just that! All she wanted was to rid her mind of the man, lose the old pain, and because she was a simple woman she had to make her forgiveness tangible, so she went to tell him personally.

I was amazed, because I grew up with the conviction that you must never let anybody else get the better of you. An eye for an eye! I used to be proud of the fact that I was often filled with revenge. When I was about thirty-five, I was despicably betrayed by a colleague. I was totally confused and incredibly angry and hurt. After I had given him a piece of my mind, I realised that, if I didn't want to drag this around with me for years on end, I would have to forgive him. I realised too that I had had my share in the affair and that he, too, was only human.

I think that is forgiveness. You don't pretend it's good, you don't forget it, you've learned a lesson, and avoid the person in future. You accept what has happened (take hold of it as it were) and then you let it go. It all takes place in your own head. It is a decision. The connection with the other person, not love but hate, is what occupies your mind and poisons you and your life, what costs you time and energy and what keeps you handcuffed to the other person. The chain has to go.

It succeeded. Immediately after all the problems, I wanted to kill him and I thought I would remain angry for the rest of my days. But no, after just a few weeks I could even give him a nod when I met him in town. I didn't become angry. I was free. Otherwise I would have remained chained to him in anger and the pain would have remained.

Forgiving somebody else is a gift to yourself and has nothing to do with that other person.

TIPS

- Who are you angry at or what has made you bitter? What has happened to you in your life that regularly springs to mind and makes you angry or sad?
- Do you want to remain a victim for the rest of your life? Do you want to give the power over your life to the person that hurt you? Do you want to remain handcuffed in anger to the perpetrator? Make a decision.
- Go and sit somewhere quiet or take a walk and repeat out loud (and mean it): "I accept you as you are / what happened and I let you / it go."

43 SELF-KNOWLEDGE

"I'm perfectly aware of who I am"

At first glance, it may seem that I am a reasonably opinionated person, and perhaps I am compared to other people, but I have never really known who I was or what I wanted. And I didn't know that I didn't know. I just muddled along.

My life was a reaction to everything and everybody. At home, they wanted me to live in a certain way and that's what I did. Or I did quite the reverse. But it was always a positive or negative reaction to my surroundings. I never thought up anything myself. At home, it was normal to study, and that's exactly what I did. And so I ruined years of my life by studying; it wasn't right for me, and certainly not at that age.

Before I started thinking about who I was and what I really wanted, I fortunately didn't have children, but I did have a profession and a relationship. At that time, I said that I had chosen everything, but in retrospect those were decisions that I had reached in a fraction of a second. Things that suited my family, my environment, and my generation. Were they really decisions?

If you start thinking about who you are and what you want, you can have some unexpected surprises. Why am I so angry and cynical? Why do I hide my emotions? Should I continue doing this? Can the suffering stop? Is this the work I really want to do for the rest of my life? What sort of person am I really? That last one in particular was a strange question for me.

How painful it is to realise that you don't want children – if you already have three. And how painful it is to realise when you're fifty that you have spent half your life in a city / church / party / profession / association just because your parents did that. How painful to accept that you are gay, after sixty. And how painful to realise when you are eighty that you have never at any time in your life paid attention to your greatest dream.

And so it was quite late before I discovered that I really wanted to be a completely different person. That I wanted different work and a different relationship, first with myself and then with others. If you don't know who you are and therefore do not have a relationship with yourself, it is extremely difficult to have anything but superficial relationships with others. But what did I want? Who was I?

Discovering who you are and what you want is a long and difficult but rewarding path. You are no longer obliged to do a lot of things. And you can decide to do other things instead. There is clarity. I really don't want to torment myself anymore. I don't want to mix with that person. I absolutely don't want to feel like that anymore. The secret passion has now been promoted to number one!

If you don't know who you are and what you want, you are the way other people want you to be, and do things that others want you to do. That's the way most people live. So, discover who you are and what you want. And do it.

Don't live the life of somebody else, live your own.

TIPS

- Learn to know yourself by asking yourself what makes you happy time and time again. What can people wake you in the middle of the night for? And what feels like a duty?
- If you were to choose that city / church / party / profession / association again, what would it be? Force yourself to answer these questions within a minute.
- You discover your greatest dream by being silent and asking yourself something. Every night before you go to bed, question yourself: What is my wildest dream? Dream about whatever you like. It can be anything!

44 OPPORTUNITIES

"Everybody gets opportunities except me"

You sometimes hear somebody say that she thinks it a pity that she has never met the right partner. Or that he has never found that wonderful job. Pity? Such people often have something desperate that they would rather not show. (Showing desperation is taboo.)

I am secretly desperate. When will I finally get my big chance? How long will I have to wait? Everybody gets rich except me. Why do I keep missing out? Everybody is successful except me. When will I ever be happy? On a sunny terrace I see everybody with sunglasses and shorts laughing together with their hip friends and raising their glasses. I cycle past them with a lump in my throat.

I would love, for example, to become a writer. Where is the publisher that phones me up? Don't they think I'm good enough? Regularly I meet people who encourage me and even offer to introduce me to a publisher. But nothing happens.

I have a friend and there's nothing wrong with him. He says that he would really like to have a girlfriend. All his friends have wives. Why hasn't he got one? Don't women like him? Occasionally he meets a nice lady, but the relationship never lasts long.

I think that everybody everywhere gets every opportunity. Nobody likes to hear that – my friend doesn't like to hear it and neither do I. We think: Indeed, everybody gets chances. Except us! I would like to be a writer, but where is that understanding publisher? My friend would really like a girlfriend, but where is she?

Everybody get opportunities and you have to look at why you don't seize those opportunities. Otherwise you will continue not seeing them and, thus, not seizing them. Why don't I want to be introduced to a publisher? Because I'm afraid that it will finally become crystal clear that I am a bad writer. It has nothing to do with publishers but with my fear of failure.

Why doesn't my friend find a girlfriend? Because he is afraid of something. Perhaps he is afraid of being vulnerable, but I know him a little and I think that he's scared that girls don't really like him and can't really love him. There are dozens, if not hundreds, of girls with whom he could have a very happy relationship. But he is so scared that it might fail that he does negative things. For example, his fear makes him very jealous, so he endlessly puts her love to the test. Or he thinks: I'll leave you before you have a chance to leave me. It has little to do with the girls and a lot to do with him.

It is a way of thinking. If you think that your publisher won't like your book or that no girl can love you, then you will (unconsciously) do everything to prove that. If you think you're not good enough, you won't see a publisher or partner even if they stand at your door. No matter how hard he knocks. And if he nevertheless gets in, you'll push him out again.

This book is an opportunity.

TIPS

- Think about an opportunity that was offered to you in the past and which you didn't seize.
- Think about why you didn't take that opportunity: What fear lies at the root of it all?
- If in the near future a chance comes along and rings your doorbell, run to the door, drag it inside, and seize that opportunity with both hands.

45 INTUITION

"What on earth caused that stomachache?"

When, around my fortieth birthday, I decided to follow my intuition, nothing happened. My whole life I had only listened to my head and others but now suddenly I expected my intuition to burst forth and tell me what on earth I should do. I was, as so often in my life, engaged in an enormous conflict with myself about something. My head and others couldn't help me. Well, my head had an opinion and others had one too, but something told me that these two had, until now, always solved things in a certain, old, fearful way, generally without success, and that hopefully there was an alternative solution, one that really worked.

Hey, there it was: "Something told me." That something was my intuition. It was covered with thick layers of dried snot and was not a welcome visitor, but fortunately it hadn't departed for good because nobody ever listened to it. I know that in my life I have sometimes taken decisions that, in retrospect, I can only say that I took because I felt that they were right. That again is my intuition.

But on the whole, I have paid little attention to my intuition. I studied law and carried on year in and year out and even completed my degree. My intuition always told me that I shouldn't on any account choose law, then that I shouldn't in any case continue with it, and then that I shouldn't spend several years finishing it. I didn't pay a blind bit of attention to all of this and so ruined years of my life.

You can hesitate between coffee with or without cream, but for all the important matters in your life you don't need to hesitate, at least not for long. Everybody knows deep down what is good for him or her and what isn't. Your intuition tells you. If you're in two minds, your fearful head is fighting against your intuition. If you don't follow your intuition, you will stay in two minds and this will cause unrest. The conflict in your mind will only disappear if you follow your intuition. If you don't listen, you won't only have unrest in your mind but also in your body. Pain in your stomach, pain in your head, pain everywhere. If you still don't listen, you will react angrily and bitterly against yourself, your surroundings, cause a traffic accident or have a heart attack.

Don't let the word meditation frighten you. When I read something about it, the coin dropped. Meditation is, I think, listening to your intuition. But in the right way, that is regularly, and according to certain rules. You eat, work, and exercise regularly and according to rules, and this is also the best way to listen to your intuition. You have to switch off your mind to what your fears and others say, so that your intuition doesn't have to try to rise above all this noise if it wants to tell you something. You can practise all that, regularly and with rules, just as you exercise. In the beginning it's extremely difficult and your mind wanders. Keep on doing it.

Your intuition tells you things. You won't always be pleased with the message, but it is what you need to hear. Listen in silence to yourself. We already know everything.

TIPS

- Find a comfortable place, turn off the telephones and the television, and take several slow deep breaths. If you are in two minds about something, repeat a sentence, for example: "I have a question and am looking for an answer."
- Every time your attention wanders to something else, quietly repeat the sentence, time and again.
- Do this at the same time every day, in the same place, and for the same length of time. The answer will come.

46 REAL

"What I secretly think"

Often in my life I have said and done something and received an answer to something completely different – namely, what I really meant. I was pleasant to my boss, but he reacted negatively. That was because I acted pleasantly towards him, but considered him a prick. He felt that and reacted to that. Or I was agreeable to a friend ("Yes, I'll lend you money") but then everything went wrong. That was because I said I wanted to lend money, but didn't really want to. My friend reacted to the latter.

For years I went to a bakery with a bitchy woman behind the counter; I took an instant dislike to her. When I saw her, I said in my mind: You really are a horrible stupid bitch! Even though I acted neutrally towards her, my daily visit to the bakery was not a pleasant experience. It wasn't my words, but perhaps my tone of voice, my look, my body language, what I didn't say (but thought) – she felt what I thought about her and she reacted to that.

I went through a period where I understood that people reacted negatively to me because I was negative. I resolved to be more positive, to say and do positive things. The result was slightly better, but nothing to write home about. People carried on reacting negatively.

Unfortunately, there is only one thing that counts: You have to really mean those positive things. The only thing that counts is what you really mean. Sooner or later, everybody feels exactly how things really are. Being surprised that people react negatively is stupid.

What should I do with the shop assistant, my boss, and that friend? I can stop having any contact with them whatsoever, but if I want to get on with them without hostility or a nasty atmosphere, then I will have to find a way of feeling really comfortable in their presence. The only way of doing that is to appreciate them for what they really do well and then see how the relationship can be improved. I should also look at what I did to create the tension, to look at my share in all this.

If I concentrate on what I think they do wrong, and thus openly or secretively have negative thoughts, I can, no, must, expect them to react negatively and I can wave goodbye to any improvement. And then I'm left with the misery.

That's the bad news. The good news is that if I exert myself and really mean the positive thoughts, remarkable things can happen. I feel better, and somebody else feels better. There is no bad atmosphere, no enmity, and no tension. If there are still negative things there is room for discussion and improvement. Life can finally begin. Thoughts are more powerful than you think. Your real, secret thoughts determine reality. In your life, you don't get what you say you want to get, but who you in the deepest recesses of your mind really are.

You reap what you really sow.

- Think about a relationship that is awkward. Do you want to continue this relationship? Then write down three good things the person does, or things that are in your interests.
- Read it every morning and evening. And also just before any contact with the person concerned. Stick it in your diary and on your refrigerator.
- Tell the person concerned.

47 POWER

"All people are equal"

In my world there were only two sorts of relationships: People I had power over and people who had power over me. I generally knew very quickly to which category every person belonged and to which I belonged. Around people over whom I had power, I felt at ease. I thought. They seemed to know better than I did what was allowed and what wasn't. They looked up to me and asked me for advice and help. I was more important than they were. They were scared and avoided any conflict with me. Apparently, they were satisfied with the way we dealt with each other.

Around people who had power over me, I didn't feel at ease. I was always very careful not to say or do anything that could spoil the person's mood. I was scared of these people and avoided any conflict. They had, by the way, not taken the power over me, it was rather that

I had given it to them. They were people who were older or acted that way, who were strict, superior, or well-known, who were more intelligent and wealthier, who were bossy and irritable.

My mother was my most important parent and she had power over me. She wasn't really bossy and irritable, but implacable; she never had any doubt (nor did I) that what she wanted would take place. I imitated that mechanism and allowed it to rule my life. I acted the child around people who had power over me, people of whom I was afraid. And with people over whom I had power, who were afraid of me, I played my mother. I always thought that the powerful were not afraid and that's why they had power over the frightened powerless.

When I became conscious of all this, I discovered that the powerful are just as frightened as the powerless. The powerless are scared that they will not gain the approval of the powerful and will do anything to get it. But the powerful are scared of being overpowered and therefore have to have power over the others. They are scared of losing power, losing control, scared of the chaos, scared to be dominated and that's why they think it is necessary to dominate people and situations.

And so everybody is scared. Nobody enjoys being scared of the person who is his boss. Just as nobody enjoys being scared of chaos. It is painful to behave as a frightened slave, just as it is painful to play the boss over such a scared slave. Sooner or later, the slave will become angry and will rebel against the boss. And the boss will become drunk with power and he will look down on the slave and start to humiliate him. If you have such a relationship with your partner, then you have a problem because power and intimacy are mutually exclusive. If you have such a relationship with yourself, you are both master and slave ("Do this! Do that!" "Yes, sure, okay, okay, fine!")

Is there no relationship possible between people without power and fear? Without masters and slaves? You have outer power and inner power. The first is having a title or uniform, forcing your will on somebody else, blackmail, hierarchy, having to be right and dominance. The second is having experience and knowledge, controlling the situation because you know what you are doing and then organising things calmly and persuasively. The first way is seizing power over others, the second is having power over yourself.

People are masters and slaves because they have no power over themselves. You get power over yourself by deciding who you really are, what you really want, and what your boundaries are. Then you don't need to seize power over others and you are not afraid of others who want to dominate you.

You can never have real power over others, only over yourself. This power over yourself brings peace and clarity, and everything surprisingly becomes better, faster, and more pleasant.

TIPS

- Is there somebody in your circle of whom you are afraid, who plays the master? React time and time again by saying that you don't like bossy people, that you find the tone irritating and that you don't like being forced to do things.
- Is there somebody in your circle who is afraid of you, over whom you want to play the master? React time and time again by saying to yourself that you can really be quite friendly, you could use a pleasant tone, and that nobody enjoys being forced to do something.
- Ask yourself time and again in a friendly tone not to harass yourself, to use a pleasant tone to yourself because getting yourself to do something doesn't succeed through threats and insults, but through a friendly explanation.

48 SELF-LOVE

"I love ... me?"

If somebody in the past had told me that I didn't love myself, I wouldn't have understood and would have probably become angry. Do you have to love yourself then? Wasn't that arrogant and selfish? And how did you love yourself? By masturbating? Going through the day thinking about yourself with a saintly smile? Looking in the mirror and saying out loud: "I love you!"? What airy-fairy bullshit!

First, I came to understand that love wasn't so much a feeling, but a certain behaviour. Love was giving somebody else your time and attention so that he could become a better and happier individual. Self-love was, therefore, giving yourself time and attention so that you could become a happier and better individual. Self-love still sounded a little boring, but I soon understood – if I wanted to be happy – that I had a problem. Why? Well, I showed exactly the opposite of self-love. I was great at sabotaging myself, causing myself pain, and shouting at myself. If you treat yourself like that, you are doing exactly the opposite of self-love and that is self-hate, giving yourself time and attention so that you can become an unhappier individual. By behaving in this way, I hated myself. That came as a shock.

Things had to change. So, you tell me – how can I start loving myself? I must give myself time and attention in such a way that I become happier from it. That assignment was unfamiliar and took on unexpected proportions: asking myself what I really wanted, what sort of person I wanted to be and what my dreams were. If I didn't dare give an answer or tried to make up excuses, I became impatient and asked the question again.

Being patient with myself – that was another good one. I always forced myself to do things at breakneck speed. And the consequence was that I was often scared and lackadaisical. Now I must, no ... I was allowed to take the time. If you give yourself time, everything goes that much more smoothly.

Respect and admiration are two other aspects of (self-) love. Yes, I really had to learn that. For I did not respect or admire myself, not one little bit. So, I was ... important? My time was important? And what I wanted was important? I was important! And were there things I could admire about myself? That turned out to be extremely difficult, much more difficult than learning to drive a car.

If forgiveness is a component of love, I had to forgive myself for hating myself. That was quite a job. I began accepting myself exactly as I was and everything I had done, and stopped punishing myself. Love also means to criticise. But surely, I had done that all my life? Well, I'd done it in the way I had been criticised as a child – vindictively and excessively harshly. I had to criticise myself in a constructive and encouraging way.

It seems as if self-love is something you have to learn and that we have all failed to learn it. If nobody loved you in your childhood, you have nobody to imitate and have to learn things yourself. First small steps and then bigger ones.

If you don't love yourself, you hate yourself.

TIPS

- Think about how you undermine yourself and how you can help yourself. How do you undermine yourself the most? What could you put in its place?
- Repeat every morning when you wake up and every evening before you go to sleep a number of positive things about yourself. For example: I am friendly, I am intelligent, I am patient, and so on. Try to mean it, but in any case start by saying it.
- Think what you would really like to have and what you can give yourself – literally or figuratively. And give it to yourself today. Give yourself a present – a massage, a beautiful piece of clothing, a pair of shoes, a compliment. Or start by forgiving yourself.

49 WORK

"Work's fine, but I'm not going to overdo things"

When I think about my work, I feel ashamed. I'll put down here how I always used to approach my work. In the first place, I wasn't really there. I was there physically, but not mentally. There were tasks to be done and I did them with a vague reluctance. My thoughts were elsewhere. I was never enthusiastic. What on earth have they thought up this time? Oh, stupid, but okay, but first let's have a bit of a gossip, drink some coffee, stare outside, read the paper, smoke, browse the internet, prepare for my holiday, or ring some of my friends. I never had the attitude of: Hey, that's a good plan to get things going, what do you need for it? Okay, let's go for it! I lacked enthusiasm, responsibility, and most particularly pleasure in my work.

As a professional procrastinator, I always did something else first. Everything was done at the very last moment, at the moment when, if it wasn't done, disaster would strike. Sometimes that last moment came and went, but it was never my fault, there was always something or somebody else I could blame. If I could get away with it, I preferred to do nothing at all, and then I would wait until a certain task became unnecessary. Without, by the way, ever telling anybody.

What I did do was complain and gossip about colleagues and particularly about my bosses. I filled my days with this, spent endless lunches on it. Hours and hours were lavished on discontent, laziness, negativity, bitchy gossip, and boredom. I went to work with the idea that the boss was somebody I didn't take seriously. Whatever he said, I disagreed with, kept silent about it, and then secretively undermined him. "Is that really necessary? Oh, but I didn't know that." Or irritably: "Sure, sure, don't worry, everything'll be alright." I said yes but didn't do it (= passive aggressive).

What I did was to become expert in skiving off. It's amazing that I kept my job, that I wasn't fired or that nobody complained to me. If I yet again stayed home ill, I received concerned messages asking me how I was. That was very sweet of my colleagues and bosses. But they should for once have told me the truth and sent me packing.

Perhaps that would have woken me up. That would have certainly been in my own best interests, because this attitude to work took many victims, and I was the first one of them. Working without enthusiasm is a disaster. Working but really wanting to be somewhere else is a daily hell. Gossiping about your colleagues and boss turns your work into a cesspool of negativity.

The way in which I approached my work was the way in which I approached my studies, my time at school, my whole life, and, yes, the way I approached myself. Without responsibility, without enthusiasm, without pleasure.

Like so many others.

TIPS

- Look for work that suits you, that you enjoy and actively look for ways of making it as pleasant as possible. Try to make your work into something that you look forward to when you wake up in the morning. Work can be so enjoyable that you forget time. People call that "flow", and you can try to achieve this in every activity.
- If you are bored, work faster and try to develop new skills.
- Don't try to do less, try to do more than what is asked. You will enjoy your work much more.
- Immediately stop procrastinating, gossiping, not taking the boss seriously, only being half present, and thus poisoning the atmosphere.

50 DO IT

"Honest, I promise!"

Once I really understood the many ways I was screwing up my life, the insights became clearer and more important for me. Something had been set into motion that couldn't be stopped. I had only one thing left to do: put these insights into practice. Actions speak louder than words. That was the ultimate test of whether I took the insights and myself seriously. But then, taking myself seriously was part of the problem.

One of the things I had to unlearn was not immediately feeling hurt if I was rejected. It took a vast amount of effort to stop wallowing in thoughts such as: You see, you've been rejected because you really are nothing! And: What right has this person to reject me! It took enormous self-discipline for me to stop these thoughts by replacing them with new ones. Sentences such as "No, this is because this particular person happens to think this way about this tiny part of you, but that doesn't immediately mean that he is right and it certainly doesn't mean you're worthless" had to be repeated time and time again until they started sounding less phoney and artificial.

I had to understand a certain principle, with my mind, before I could do something about it. At the same time, understanding what is painful is in itself so liberating that you could almost forget that it is followed by another necessary step – namely putting it into practice. That last step is the hardest. It is not familiar; you can fail and have the inclination to be impatient, to ridicule yourself and immediately punish yourself if it doesn't go without a hitch. Don't do that!

Falling back into old habits happened and happens constantly. Particularly when there is little time, when there are tensions, when there is conflict. Falling back used to make me feel defeated, but that passes. I am allowed to make many mistakes, as long as I realise it, and if, the next time, circumstances allow, I do it right. Or otherwise the time after next.

I noticed tensions in my environment. Thinking and talking about these things, that's fine, but actually doing something about them is taking things just a bit too far. People want you to be the way you've always been, with all your ill will and self-hate and lack of patience with them. They prefer the old familiar invalid to the new, unfamiliar healthy person.

I also noticed that birds of a feather flock together. When I was angry, I was surrounded by angry people. If you change, you will notice that some grumpy friends and acquaintances may disappear. They will be replaced by less angry people.

It is like learning a foreign language. I had to work at it for years on end in my head, practise it on my own, read about it, think about it, repeat it and also unlearn a lot. Putting it into practice starts with speaking, stuttering, stammering a few words. In the end, you talk and think in such a way that it becomes your first language.

It is your daily behaviour that tells you who you really are, what you really think, and what and particularly who you really love.

Out of 100 people who read this book, 99 will do nothing. But that one person is going to experience something remarkable.

TIPS

- Don't wait until you feel like it or for that day when you have time for it. That day will never come. Do it today; do it now. The path to hell is paved with good intentions.
- Accept and expect things to go wrong to start with. That is essential to pave the way for the one time it succeeds. The path to heaven is paved with doing and lots of failures.
- If you are a stubborn, negative, always-in-the-right tyrant such as me, doing something new and difficult is a disaster. But not doing anything is an even greater disaster.

POSTSCRIPT

Dear reader, is your head spinning from all the ways you can screw up your life? Don't forget that I have tried to understand and change each and every one of these ways, one at a time. So, don't read the chapters one after another and certainly don't try to tackle every problem at the same time. Take them one by one, as I did.

Don't rush things. I have been trying for more than ten years to do better and sometimes I succeed, but often I still don't get things right. Often something goes wrong: I deny angrily and stubbornly that I've done something wrong, something unexpected occurs, or tension causes me to forget all my good intentions. I constantly relapse into old, trusted, familiar but wrong habits of thinking and doing. Start afresh, every time, just as I do.

So select one subject and take your time. Even if you only do one thing better on one occasion, you're already a hero. My hero.

And the most important thing of all: Please don't stay there in the shit!

I hope that you have enjoyed reading this book, and have learned something. I would very much appreciate if you could possibly write a short review. That would be very helpful indeed! Thank you very much in advance!

I dedicate this book to Oprah Winfrey who opened my eyes again and again.

On Dutch television they tried forever to imitate The Oprah Winfrey Show. They weren't sure what the 'secret' of the show was. The format? The way of choosing and handling subjects? Or perhaps the style of interviewing people? No, the 'secret' of the show was... Oprah. In Holland there was, and there is, not one host who is comparable to Oprah. She has an extremely rare combination of many qualities. She is very intelligent, generous, ambitious, courageous, businesslike, hard-working, and has lots and lots of empathy. But her most important quality: she is authentic.

Oprah Winfrey has transcended her own tv show, a clear mark of quality. With her enormous influence in the US and in the dozens of countries where her daily show could be seen, she has built an empire that she uses to convey her message. Smugly people talk about "the Oprahfication of America", but it is rather the Oprahfication of the world.

What is her message? The heart of her thinking and her show is empowerment, which in fact relates to her own life story. You can crawl out of your misery and even become happy. Listen to your conscience, your intuition, your soul, your higher self, your God. You can change your life; you are the (only!) one who is responsible for your life. She writes in her book What I Know for Sure: "You become what you believe - not what you wish or want but what you truly believe. Wherever you are in life, look at your beliefs. They put you there." If you want to be a princess but you think you are a worm, then you are satisfied with the job / relationship / life of a worm. For the millions and millions of her viewers who trust her as a friend and for whom spirituality, philosophy and literature are at best vague acquaintances, this is a radical and life-changing gift.

I have worked in tv for 25 years. Years ago I visited The Oprah Winfrey Show in Chicago. After the show I tried to leave the studio but it went very slowly, since apparently there was someone at the exit who wanted to shake hands with everybody, just like in church.

When I shake hands with Oprah, I tell her that I'm from Holland. She immediately asks me: "Do you live in Amsterdam?" Regularly she gets letters from a Dutch girl in great distress. Could I possibly help this girl? After meeting the girl in Amsterdam and finding her a therapist, suddenly I receive a big envelope containing Oprah's portrait with some handwritten words and her signature.

François de Waal with picture of Oprah Winfrey.